Ideas in History

Journal of the Nordic Society
for the History of Ideas

Volume 6, no. 2

2012

Museum Tusculanum Press
University of Copenhagen

Ideas in History
Journal of the Nordic Society for the History of Ideas
© 2013 Ideas in History, Copenhagen
Cover design: Erling Lynder
ISBN 978 87 635 4106 0
ISSN 1890 1832

Editor
Ben Dorfman, Aalborg University

About the Journal
Ideas in History is the result of collaborative efforts among nearly a dozen universities and colleges throughout the Nordic countries. The purpose of these initiatives is to further awareness of research, resources and activities in the field of intellectual history in the Nordic countries as well as internationally. The journal aims to create a meeting ground for the study of ideas in historical context across disciplinary, geographical and institutional boundaries. *Ideas in History* welcomes interdisciplinary approaches to intellectual history at the same time it acknowledges specific traditions in the field. *Ideas in History* seeks a pluralism of methodological approaches to intellectual history: reflections on the field, historical contexts studied, subject matter for intellectual-historical investigation, critical understandings of relations between the intellectual past and present as well as the comprehension of culturally, politically and geographically diverse intellectual traditions.

Acknowledgements
Ideas in History is published with the financial assistance of the Nordic Board for Periodicals in the Humanities in the Humanities and Social Sciences. *Ideas in History* also wishes to thank the Department of Philosophy, Classics, History of Art and Ideas at the University of Oslo for its generous support of the editorial administration of this journal.

Manuscripts
Editorial Assistant, Ideas in History
Dept. of Culture and Global Studies Aalborg University
Kroghstræde 3
DK-9220 Aalborg East, Denmark
Email ideasinhistory@cgs.aau.dk

Subscription
Museum Tusculanum Press
University of Copenhagen
Njalsgade 126
DK-2300 Copenhagen S, Denmark
Tel. +45 35 32 91 09 / Fax +45 35 32 91 13
Email order@mtp.dk / www.mtp.dk

Contents

Note from the Editor's Desk

Ben Dorfman, editor

The following issue of *Ideas in History* encompasses a special issue on the history of economic thought, plus a provocative paper taking on issues of text, historiography and deconstructive thought in cultural history. We look forward to readers deriving rich rewards from the diverse range of papers in this issue.

Introduction
The Intellectual History of Economic Thought

Jakob Bek-Thomsen, Mikkel Thorup, Christian Olaf Christiansen and Stefan Gaarsmand Jacobsen[1]

In his *Second Treatise on Government* from 1690, John Locke said that the same laws of nature which gives us property "bound that Property too". One is not free to use one's property in any possible way and still maintain it as one's own property. Property right has enabling as well as constraining faculties. This fits with a foundational claim of intellectual history; namely, that all statements both facilitate and limit action. One can only do that which one can also explain and legitimate as a reasonable form of behaviour, and that legitimization constrains one's possible contemporary and future actions. That is, at least if one's actions are to be seen as legitimate.

While this claim of intellectual history have mainly been used to investigate the history of political thought, the purpose of this themed section of *Ideas in History* is to further an ongoing but nonetheless limited orientation towards an intellectual histories of economic ideas and economic life more broadly. We want to suggest that economic reasoning is a fertile field for intellectual history which has been too often left to economic historians and economists—this perhaps due to the degree of mathematical reasoning in neoclassical economy or to a sheer "fear of numbers" in the humanities.

Applying this foundational claim to the history of economic reasoning, we may easily appreciate that what counts as legitimate economic activity, whether it concerns company profit-making, bank business, household labour, begging, etc., is highly historical contingent. The economic practice of slavery, for instance, has become impossible to justify. Profit-making, on the other

1 Mikkel Thorup is associate professor in the Department of Culture and Society, Program for Philosophy and History of Ideas, Aarhus University. Jakob Bek-Thomsen is assistant professor in the Department of Culture and Society, Program for Philosophy and History of Ideas, Aarhus University. Christian Olaf Christiansen is assistant professor in the Department of Culture and Society, Program for Philosophy and History of Ideas, Aarhus University. Stefan Gaardsmand Jacobsen is assistant professor in the Department of Culture and Society, Program for Philosophy and History of Ideas, Aarhus University. The editors of this theme section are all engaged in the research project "Economic Argumentation: Conflicts between Economy, Religion and Natural Science as Knowledge- and Practice-authorities" (see http://ecora.au.dk/), a work made possible through a grant from the Velux Foundation.

hand, seems to have altered its status from being ill-regarded, partly due to religious beliefs, to have become a norm in itself, which again has become challenged from a broad range of, e.g., social and environmental concerns. In brief, economic reasoning and practice is historically embedded.

Enlarging the meaning of "economic," we want to argue that the history of economic thought is more than the history of the economy and economists. "Economy" is not only something that is, but also something we do, say and think. Economy is arguments, perceptions and actions. Going from "the economy" to economic reasoning, we see that economic reasoning is embedded in ideas, practices, cultural codes, behavioral norms, religious prohibitions, societal and institutional conventions, scientific standards, jokes, aesthetic products etc. Economic reasoning plays out in the totality of human physical and mental productions. It is not limited to tabulations of GDP, inflation rates or profit margins. It is also not restricted to professional economists or bankers. Economic reasoning is something we all do, constantly testing, describing and explaining our behavior using economic models and metaphors or using non-economic languages to describe our market behavior. As Michael Sandel demonstrates in his 2012 book, *What Money Can't Buy*, economic reasoning is both highly influenced non-economic standards of evaluation and is thoroughly historical. There is in a sense no such thing as *the* economy. There is only and endlessly changing flux of people doing, thinking and speaking what they take to be economically, creating economies as they go along.

Economic reasoning is historical contingent, dependent upon contemporary cultural, philosophical, scientific, religious standards; filled with metaphors, images, models, concepts borrowed from outside economics; part of society's struggles over the proper codes of evaluation; part of the societal identification, naming and owning of "problems" and their solutions; engaged in constant practices of 'authorization' and discursive constructions of the "true," "proper," "profitable," "legitimate;" a historical, changeable way of knowing, writing, demonstrating, advising, encouraging, prohibiting; and therefore to be found also outside "pure" economics and economic transaction. We believe that these historical and cultural characteristics of economic reasoning, often involving questions of meaning, discourse, legitimacy, rhetoric, use of language and metaphors, show that intellectual history has much to offer for an in-depth understanding of the role economic thinking, reasoning, concepts, etc., play and have played in societies, then and now.

The contributions to this theme section demonstrate, in each their way, how intellectual historians can go about studying the history of economic ideas. One point to note is that such histories do not have to revolve around the theories of "big economic thinkers," but can trace economic reasoning and discourse at various levels. Further, the section shows that the contexts for understanding "big economic thoughts" must be expanded beyond the imagery of an isolated and timeless community of fellow economists.

Christian Olaf Christiansen, in his article "From 'The History of Economic Thought' to 'Economic Intellectual History,'" argues that whereas key contributions to economic intellectual history can indeed be found back in the 1970s, much history of economic thought have been written by economists, and centered on telling the tale of the "big economic thinkers." However, two recent developments have opened up new venues for economic intellectual history. First, there is the broadening of the scope of intellectual history, opening up new possibilities concerning the where, when, what, who, and how of intellectual history. Second, there are notable developments outside of intellectual history, as in economic sociology and anthropology, whose contributions to the study of economic ideas may contribute to the further development of economic intellectual history. The article maps different genres of economic intellectual history. It distinguishes, first, between, analytical and historical reconstructions, and it then moves on to demonstrate how the study of economic ideas can be found within different genres of intellectual history, such as conceptual history, genealogical studies, and linguistic pragmatism. The article provides an overview of the field of economic intellectual history, categorizes several main approaches, and it outlines possible future directions.

Reopening an eighteenth century *locus classicus* for the history of economic thought, Stefan Gaarsmand Jacobsen explores the concept of natural order as it was used by Francois Quesnay and Adam Smith in their respective economic writings. The article argues for a reassessment of these famous writings that excludes any teleological interpretations of the theories as having reached a modern and scientific understanding of economic mechanisms ahead of their time. Their use of natural order in the context of political economy provides a lens through which Smith's and Quesnay's metaphysical, religious and normative foundations become clearer. While Smith used the concept only after having visited Quesnay and the physiocrats in France in the 1760s, in *The Wealth of Nations* he sought to negotiate the meaning of what was "natural" about economic life. The physiocrats believed it possible to identify a model or a perfect regime of natural order—an order that they in fact thought to exist and function in China due to a rigorous system of economic laws. Smith sided with contemporary critics of this metaphysical vision of economic perfection (and of Chinese governance), but he suggested that the economic mechanisms of the physiocratic theories would remain intact even with a minimum of control by state laws. However, Smith's balancing act on these questions remained disputed even by his Scottish successors in political economy, and the problem of ordering the society from the vantage point of an economic science was rephrased as a problem of combining the physiocratic metaphysics of natural order with the 'business of the world' as expounded by Smith.

Joseph Malherek's "Qualitative Capitalism and Continental Critique: Émigré Social Scientists Encounter the American Consumer, 1933–45" is an intellectual biography of the socialist and social scientist Paul Lazersfeld (1901–76), describing Lazersfeld's early career in the US from 1933–45. Lazersfeld, a Viennese born Emigrant to the United States, used his skills in mathematics and psychology to develop empirical social research, which were used in marketing and market research. It was also instrumental, so Malherek argues, in developing social empirical studies at the emigrée Frankfurt School. Surprisingly, then, socialism, theories of human motivation, and theories of social stratification were used for marketing and market research purposes. As Malherek writes, this study "demonstrates the creative application of socialist and psychoanalytic insights to capitalism's problems with its mysterious markets." In sum, this biographical study of Lazarsfeld and his mid-century social science US environment, tells the story of the socialist and psychological origins of market research.

From the "History of Economic Thought" to "Economic Intellectual History"

Christian Olaf Christiansen[1]

Abstract

In the midst of a world in severe economic, financial, and unemployment crisis, this article seeks to examine what economic intellectual history is and what it has been, and what it might be in the process of becoming. Economic intellectual history as a sub-field of intellectual history has been flourishing at least since the 1970s, but it has not been given as much attention as, e.g., the history of political thought. This is partly because much history of economic thought has been written by economists, trained in the techniques of economics. Taking notice of two recent developments, one inside intellectual history, and one outside of it, this article seeks to show how economic intellectual history is, and increasingly can be, something different than "the history of economic thought," economist-style. The first development is the broadening of intellectual history. This relates to its now many available methodologies, its expansions in relation to time, space, actors and sources it can study. This broadening has important consequences for economic intellectual history. The article thus maps how different genres of intellectual history, such as conceptual history, genealogical studies, etc., already deal specifically with the histories of economic concepts, discourse, and ideas. The second development refers to the many recent contributions of the study of economic discourse, ideas, reasoning, etc., which have been developed in other disciplines than intellectual history, such as economic sociology, anthropology, etc., that economic intellectual history can draw upon. The article uses and develops categorizations of economic intellectual history which will hopefully be useful for orientation in a broad field, distinguishing between historical and rational reconstructions of economic thinking, mapping out various approaches to economic intellectual history, such as histories of legitimization, and outlining some possible future perspectives.

1 Christian Olaf Christiansen is assistant professor in the Department of Culture and Society, Program for Philosophy and History of Ideas, Aarhus University. This article was made possible through funding from the Velux Foundation.

Introduction: Intellectual History and its Relation to Economic Intellectual History

In a recent review of professional historians' study of the history of economic life in the last thirty years, economic historian William H. Sewell, Jr. (2010, 147) concludes that there has been a relative neglect of the history of economic life: "Precisely in the years since 1980, when globalization, deindustrialization, repeated financial crises, and soaring economic inequality should have made obvious the need for a deeper historical understanding of modern capitalism's dynamism and perversity, historians have largely abandoned the historical study of economic life while economists turned economic history into a branch of mathematical development economics." This neglect is paradoxical, because, as Sewell explains, the time is more than ripe for a revitalization of the study of economic life. Whereas Sewell's article is on the *history* profession in the United States and its apparent neglect of the study of the history of economic life, this article asks whether a similar "paradoxical situation" is an apt description of *intellectual history*. Intellectual history is a particular historical discipline with its own research objects, methods, and aims that are *not* simply identical to those of historians *per se*. To which degree has intellectual history been preoccupied with the history of *economic* ideas?

On the one hand, topics related to the historical study of economic ideas and argumentations do not figure prominently in intellectual history journals such as *Journal of the History of Ideas*.[2] Intellectual history as a discipline has not had the history of economic ideas and arguments as its main area of research, at least not when compared to e.g. the interest in the history of political thought, which for a long time seems to have been the favourite subject of intellectual history.[3] On the other hand, many intellectual histories of capitalism and of economic ideas have been written since the late 1970s.[4] For example, there is now a substantial revisionist scholarship on Adam Smith (e.g., Rothschild 2001; Winch 1978). According to American intellectual historian Richard F. Teichgraeber III, remarkable work in intellectual history

---

2 This is at least what is indicated from a minor survey on the database *Web of Science*. Searching in the journals *Journal of the History of Ideas, Modern Intellectual History* and *History of European Ideas* yielded a total result of more than 6000 articles, but less than 100 (91) were related to economic intellectual history, as indicated by searching for the key words "economic thought," "political economy," "capitalism" and "economics." A more comprehensive survey, however, would also include other intellectual history journals such as *Intellectual History Newsletter, Intellectual History Review, Redescriptions, Modern Intellectual History, Contributions* and *Ideas in History*, but these journals are not included in the *Web of Science* bibliometric database.

3 On the dominance of the history of political ideas, see, e.g., Collini (2012) or Gordon (2012).

4 For assessments of this development, cf., e.g., Teichgraeber (2004) or Sklansky (2012).

came out in the decades after the challenge from the rise of social history, often on shifting historical views on capitalism. If the history of economic ideas has been given somewhat less attention than, e.g., the history of political thought, then, there are surely very notable exceptions.[5] Still, however, one reason why the history of economic ideas has not been as prominent a feature of intellectual history as the history of political thought, is that the history of economic thought has primarily been someone else's discipline, namely that of trained economists.

This article is an investigation of *economic* intellectual history. Where do we find economic intellectual history? Within intellectual history and its different branches or genres, where do we find examples of work which is mainly preoccupied with the history of *economic* thought, discourse, and argumentation? Studies of economic intellectual history date back to at least the 1970s. This article traces examples of economic intellectual history from within genres such as conceptual history, genealogical intellectual history, science studies, etc. The article categorizes different approaches to economic intellectual history. As intellectual history recently seems to have expanded its scope, this is also reflected in the study of economic intellectual history, as, e.g., in attempts to move beyond the study of "the great economists," and in attempts to make more use of contributions of neighbouring disciplines such as economic sociology. Economic intellectual history already is, and should be, much more than "history of economic thought," and new developments both within and outside intellectual history demonstrate further promising developments for economic intellectual history.

History of Economic Thought: Who Solved the Problems of Economic Theory?

An investigation of what "economic intellectual history" has been, currently is, and how it might possibly develop further, should start by paying attention to a genre which has developed and cultivated partly *outside* the discipline of intellectual history. There is thus already a strongly established, and seem-

---

5 Exceptions include e.g. the works of the Sussex-based intellectual historian (and originally trained economist) Donald Winch, cf., his 1996 book, *Riches and Poverty: An Intellectual History of Political Economy in Britain, 1750–1834*. There is a special issue of *History of European Ideas* on "Economic Concepts and European Thought in Historical Perspective" from 1988. Some (arbitrary) examples of economic intellectual history published in intellectual history journals include e.g. Morley 1998, arguing that Antique political economy did play a major role in the rise of modern (eighteenth century) political economy; Walter (2008) argues that J.G.A. Pocock stretches the term "political economy" too much when it is applied to seventeenth century "economic" thinking. Cf. also Teichgraeber (2004, 267) for a list of seminal contributions.

ingly currently expanding, field of the *history of economic thought*. History of economic thought investigates the history of economic ideas and arguments, but it is especially concerned with the history and the development of economic *theory*. Often, as we shall see, this is connected to debates around who contributed to economic theory and in which way. Main journals include *History of Political Economy* (1969), *History of Economics Review* (1973), *Research in the History of Economic Thought and Methodology* (1983), *European Journal of the History of Economic Thought* (1993) and *History of Economic Ideas* (1993).[6] According to historian of economic thought Marc Blaug, it is mostly economists with historical interests (and often "heterodox economists,") who contribute, suggesting that much history on economic thinking is not done by intellectual historians, but by people trained in economics. According to another prominent historian of economic thought, Denis P. O'Brien, training in economics is necessary because acquaintance with economic techniques is a condition for understanding economic analysis.[7]

Traditionally, it has thus often been trained economists who have written the histories of economic thought.[8] One obvious reason for this seems to be the very nature of the subject matter. Ever since the sophisticated usage of mathematics and econometrics became commonplace in economics, it has been increasingly difficult for non-economists to comprehend these highly technical debates.[9] Economics has, we may note in the passing, become a master, or expert, discourse.[10]

In line with the current argument here, we should note that economics (political economy) has often had natural science as its scientific (epistemological and methodological) ideal. Ever since the late nineteenth century and

---

6 This list of journals is taken from Blaug (2001).

7 O'Brien's (2007) work on the history of economic thought is described as an "intellectual discipline," *not* as an "intellectual history" that sees the development of economics in a wider intellectual context. It is thus, as we shall see, comparable to Schumpeter's idea of a history of *economic analysis*. Cf. the book review by Backhouse (2008).

8 Some of the perhaps most prominent not contemporary examples of trained economists and their writings on the history of economic thought would include, e.g., Galbraith (1987), Heilbroner (1953), and Schumpeter (1954).

9 According to Blaug (2001, 161), there has been an "explosion" in books on the history of econometrics since the late 1980s.

10 This is a development which stands in a remarkable (and some would say disturbing) contrast to the embedding of nation states economies into a globalized economy. Few people are offered any chance of understanding of the workings of the global economy, whereas most people are certainly affected by it. The ideological belief that modern human beings are "masters of their own fate" has become increasingly naive (if it ever was not); instead, their existence is conditioned upon the play of global economic forces, towards which most are not only powerless, but blinded, since the economic and financial processes are highly complex.

the so-called *Methodenstreit* of economics, mainstream economic science has been nomothetic rather than ideographic. That is, it has been concerned with the discovery of laws and regularities rather than with meaning and understanding of individual historical phenomena. It has been concerned with the development of a true science of the economy, which would increasingly be able to explain, and predict, economic facts. This criterion, i.e., the question of which theory does the best job in explaining economic facts, has consequences when applied to the *history* if economic thought. Indeed, economists have often looked at the history of economic thought this way: history is mostly interesting if it can shed light on the improvement of economics as a science, on who was wrong and who was right, and hence still of some use.

This seems traditionally, as well as currently, to be the case. It is true when it comes to classical political economy: Adam Smith or David Ricardo, for instance, do not seem to be interested in the history of political economy *per se*, but only in order to judge which theory has performed the best in solving economic (if not at the same time moral and political) problems. It is also true when it comes to the greatest critic of classical political economy, Karl Marx: he engages in a discussion with other political economists to prove them wrong, and to develop his own theory.[11] This is the traditional stance for reading the history of economic thought; i.e., which theory did or did not contribute to the understanding of economic (if not social, political or moral) problems.

Schumpeter's History of "Economic Analysis"

Perspectives emphasizing the problem of who contributed to understanding economic "problems" seems only to have gained more momentum ever since "economics" became the preferred substitute term for "political economy." A key note in the academic field of the history of economic thought is Austrian economist Joseph A. Schumpeter's *History of Economic Analysis*, published posthumously in 1954. Schumpeter's work can with some right be said to belong to a genre which might be called "The Great Books of Economists."[12] This genre often involves a struggle concerning the canonical list of key contributions to the development of economics as a science, around who is to be part of such a

---

11 Cf., for examples, Adam Smith's discussion of Quesnay: Smith (2009, 435ff), Ricardo's (2004, 5–13) discussion of, e.g., Adam Smith, or the numerous examples of Karl Marx (1990) discussing the works of various political economists.

12 The genre may be compared to the history of philosophy: for similar reasons why most philosophers would probably be sceptical of non-philosophers writing the history of philosophy, economists are sceptical of non-economists writing the history of economic thought.

canon, and who contributed with what. Most (if not all) histories of economic thought would include, e.g., Smith, Marx and Keynes in their books. But their contribution in respect to improving economic analysis will be judged differently. A main principle of observation is thus the question of *who* contributed to economic theory, a discussion of the value of economic thought in different periods of history, and of different economic schools and doctrines. If far-reaching, such an exposition of the history of economic thought goes back to antiquity (especially Aristotle, but partly also Plato and Xenophon), and then typically works its way up to the present day through scholastic economic thinking, mercantilism, the physiocrats, classical political economy, Marxism and socialism, neo-classical economics and the marginal revolution, Keynesianism, monetarism, and so forth.[13] This kind of endeavour (writing a "canon" of the most important economic thinkers) then leads to quarrels about who should or should not be included into the history of economic thought, or about from which "yardstick" other economists' work should be measured.[14]

Writing a history of economic thought relies, whether implicit or explicit, on principles for observation. For our purposes, we should notice how carefully Schumpeter distinguishes "history of economic *analysis*" from a "history of systems of economic thought" or a "history of economic thought":

> It would, I suppose, be possible to write alongside a history of economic analysis another history of the popular views of economic subjects. By the same token it is possible to write a history of economic thought that traces out the historical change of attitudes, mentioning analytic performances in passing. Such a history would indeed display the close association that exists within the attitudes of the public mind in the sense defined, with the kind of problems that as any given time interest analysts and form

---

13 Some notable recent contributions to such a comprehensive "history of economic thought" would include, e.g., Blaug (1997); Perlman and McCann (2000); O'Brien (2007); Roncaglia (2006); Rothbard (1995). For a short history of economic thought, see Sandelin, Trautwein and Wundrak (2008).

14 For example, William J. Barber in his review of Allessandro Roncaglio's recent key contribution to the history of economic thought, *The Wealth of Ideas: A History of Economic Thought*, claims that Roncaglia uses the works of economist Piero Sraffa as "the benchmark against which competing theories are evaluated" (Barber 2007, 552). Some recent examples of debates about who should be included into the canon of economic thought are e.g. Becker (2008), arguing that American writer Henry David Thoreau should be included into the history of economic thought because of his non-instrumentalist view on nature; Michaelides et al. (2011), arguing that ancient Greek philosopher Democritus has been much overlooked in the history of economic thought, as he had 'anticipated' many later developments.

the general attitude or spirit in which they approach their problems. Our own plan is exactly the opposite one (Schumpeter 1954, 39).

Schumpeter chose to focus upon a history of economic thought centered on the history of economic *analysis*, not on "the popular views of economic subjects" or the "general attitude or spirit," trying to "disentangle analytical work from its popular background." Ultimately, Schumpeter is interested in contributions to economic analysis, that is, to the science of economics.

From this perspective, today's science easily becomes the point of view from which the historical observer judges earlier thinking. Economic thinking is portrayed as a science which has been trying to answer 'eternal questions' such as what is money, what is value, etc. By this account, Aristotle's theory of money is simply wrong, unfulfilling, and of limited interest. This way of approaching economic thinking—as the history of economic analysis or, as we shall see, as "rational reconstruction," is also what we often find in the present day academic discipline of the history of economic thought. As Mark Blaug writes, it can be difficult for economists to read, e.g., Marx "un-analytically:" "Why did the poor fellow [Marx] try to attribute the value of the product to a single output, labor, without knowing anything about marginal productivity?" (Blaug 2001, 151). Marx's economic thinking is dismissed because it was simply wrong, as it was written before the neo-classical concept of marginal utility had been introduced. Blaug refers back to Schumpeter as he distinguishes between *analytical* and *historical* reconstructions. Whereas the first is equated with economic analysis, the latter is described as "the relationship of economic theory to economic policy, the influence of social, philosophical and political preconceptions on the development [of] economic ideas, the methodological views of the great economists, the sociology of the economics profession, the international diffusion of economic ideas, and similar wide-ranging questions about the history of ideas as applied to economics" (Blaug 2001, 149–50).[15] According to Blaug, himself a proponent of historical reconstructions, "some historians of economic thought have tried to sell the subject to their departmental colleagues" by focusing upon "rational reconstructions," since economists typically have had low thoughts about the use of historical knowledge about economics (Blaug 2001, 150). As the scientific and epistemological ideal of much economics is natural science, it can take on the same view on the value of history. A science in progress is one which

15 Blaug's distinction between analytical and historical reconstruction relies upon the distinction made by Richard Rorty (1984) in his seminal article.

can, ultimately, *forget* its history. Blaug explains why many mainstream economists have little faith in the value of history, hence the title of the article, and
why it thus for many historians of economic thought has been tempting to
write analytical instead of historical reconstructions.[16]

Getting beyond the History of Economic Thought, Schumpeter-Style

We should pause at this distinction being made between "rational" (in Schumpeter's sense of "economic analysis") and "historical" reconstruction. Most
intellectual historians would probably find themselves more familiar (and
comfortable) with "historical reconstructions." Whereas, e.g., Blaug's conception of the history of economic thought is mostly concerned with great thinkers and great theories, also when he traces new developments of the history of
economic thought, I would suggest that economic intellectual history encompasses a larger range of possible subjects of inquiry—economic ideas, arguments, rhetoric, and discourse. Economic intellectual history investigates how
historical actors or historical discourse make sense and give meaning to "economic life." It should not be confined to economic theory. And even if it was
to concentrate solely on the contribution of "great thinkers" or intellectuals
to economic discourse, which isn't necessary, it can easily go beyond the contribution of (political) economists to the thinking done by sociologists (such
as Max Weber), or anthropologists (such as Bronislaw Malinowski or Karl
Polanyi).[17] The point is that much theorizing or thinking of "the economy" is
done by other academics than economists. Economists do not have an exclusive right to economic theorization, and an economic intellectual history can
go beyond the study of economists and political economists.

---

16 Blaug critiques rational reconstructions that anachronistically put words into historical actors'
mouths that they don't have. He ultimately justifies the study of the history of economic thought
by the idea that the development of economics is *path-dependent*: "no idea or theory in economics,
physics, chemistry, biology, philosophy and even mathematics is ever thoroughly understood except
as the end-product of a slice of history, the result of some previous intellectual development" (Blaug
2001, 156). Blaug thus concludes that "the history of economic thought is not a specialization within
economics. It is economics—sliced vertically against the horizontal axis of time" (Blaug 2001, 157). In
the end, then, although Blaug strongly positions "historical reconstruction" as opposed to "analytic
reconstructions," he does remain mainly interested in the development of economics as a science as
being the defining contribution of the history of economic thought. One point I make in this article
is that this restriction does not apply to what I have here labelled "economic intellectual history." That
is, for economic intellectual history, the development of economics as a science is only one possible
inquiry amongst many others.

17 For an assessment of the contribution of economic anthropology, cf., e.g., Gregory (2009, 285).
Is it not also telling, for instance, that e.g. a political economy reader (Barma and Vogel 2008)
refers to anthropologists, sociologists, political scientists and historians *as well as to economists* as key
contributors to the intellectual history of political economy?

We should note that historicizing economic ideas, arguments, and discourse, has also been done from other academic disciplines, perspectives, methodologies, observational criteria, etc., than those narrowly defined by the "history of economic thought" approach. Furthermore, historicizing economic ideas and discourse has been done by intellectual historians as well as by disciplines such as cultural history, history of science, and (economic) sociology. My suggestion is that "economic intellectual history" has as much to gain from these studies as from the history of economic analysis, Schumpeter style. There is much to learn from, e.g., studies following in the lines of Michel Foucault and discourse theory, from recent developments in economic sociology, or from historical-constructivist histories of economic theory—although these studies do typically not label themselves as "intellectual history." (I will return to examples of research on the history of economic ideas, arguments and discourse from both "within" intellectual history, as well as from "outside" of what is typically understood as being intellectual history.)

An economic intellectual history thus self-consciously sees the "history of economic analysis" of "great economists" to be only *one* possibility amongst many others. By "economic intellectual history" is here not meant a return to "economism," if by this we mean a kind of historiography which seeks, "from the bottom up," to explain discourse, ideas, language, morality, etc., from social and economic factors. Whereas this very well might be a caricature of the social history which gained ground in the 1960s, it does need emphasis that such an attempt (explaining ideas through social and material forces), is not what is suggested here. This would also be somewhat paradoxical, since the very rise of social history "caused headaches among intellectual historians" (Bavaj 2010, 11). Whereas social history might at first has been seen as a threat, however, today there are many examples of economic intellectual history which makes use of social history, without threatening the autonomy or *raison d'être* of intellectual history (Sklansky 2012).

If anything, we might as well note what seems to be a return to the "power of ideas." As American intellectual historian Daniel Rodgers notes in his much discussed *Age of Fracture*: "Economies are rooted not only in structures of exchange but also, and just as fundamentally, in ideas, practices, norms, and conventions" (Rodgers 2011, 9). Marieke De Goede, in her Foucauldian inspired genealogy of financial discourse, even suggests that finance is "profoundly cultural" (De Goede 2005, 179). Whereas this might sound somewhat exaggerated, as an overly "idealistic" conception of economic life, the point is that distinctly cultural and historically contingent factors such as language, norms, values, knowledge, institutions, etc., condition economic life and thinking.

Returning to the topic of recent developments in intellectual history, we may first note that there has been a broadening of interest. As English intellectual historian Stefan Collini (2012, 1) writes, "the emancipation of intellectual history from domination by, or exclusive identification with, the history of political thought has been one of the most significant recent developments." According to Danish intellectual historian Mikkel Thorup (2012), intellectual historians are currently expanding the boundaries of their work. These expansions are along multiple lines: *where* (e.g., global perspectives), *when* (e.g., contemporary history), which *sources* can be used, what *objects* or themes of research, and which *actors* focused upon (e.g. marginalized voices, or "in-between-figures" such as bureaucrats etc.). Furthermore, there is now quite a broad range of approaches or methodologies available, such as genealogical intellectual history (Foucault), conceptual history (Koselleck), linguistic contextualism (the "Cambridge School"), science studies, cultural intellectual history, history of mentalities, etc.

If this broad conceptualization of intellectual history is acknowledged, that is, as an expansion of the where, the when, who, and sources of interest for intellectual historians, we may appreciate that much intellectual history of economic ideas has been written already. Both by self-acknowledged intellectual historians, as well as by people who do not identify themselves as intellectual historians, but whose work (with this broader conceptualization of intellectual history in mind) might be characterized as such, or at least as being highly relevant for intellectual history, and for further developments of economic intellectual history.

To be sure, appreciating this does require a second expansion: namely that history of economic ideas, argumentation, discourse, etc., differs from the history of economic thought narrowly understood as the canonical list of "great economists" and their contribution to "economic analysis." Instead of a history of "economic analysis" and of big economists, we then have histories of economic ideas, argumentation, discourse, etc. Instead of a narrow interest in economic thought, there is an opening towards economic thinking in relation to social and political thought. I therefore suggest distinguishing between history of economic thought and economic intellectual history. This is not, it should be stressed, to dismiss the kind of historiography associated with "history of economic thought." Rather, it is to point out other directions for intellectual history than one which consists in the history of economists thinking about the economy.

Examples of Economic Intellectual History from Different Genres of Intellectual History

We may note that just as there now exists a methodological pluralism for intellectual history in general, and a broadening of its scope, this is also, at least partly, reflected in the study of the history of economic ideas and argumentation.[18] From within each of different key areas of intellectual history, such as genealogical intellectual history, conceptual history, historical contextualism, science studies, deconstructivism/literary intellectual history, cultural intellectual history, and the history of mentality, we can take a closer look at contributions to economic intellectual history.

Genealogical intellectual history, often inspired by the work of Michel Foucault, has proved much fruitful for the study of economic intellectual history. Marieke De Goede (2005), for instance, has written a genealogy of finance which traces the shifting historical moral status of different kinds of financial activities and institutions, such as the trading of stocks, paper money, public debt, trading of futures, etc. Alex Preda, an economic sociologist often working with a historical perspective, has similarly traced the modern discourses on finance across different nations and times, highlighting the struggles for moral and legal legitimacy of financial capitalism, drawing on a vast range of empirical sources, such as "great texts" as well as pamphlets, archival research at stock exchanges, investor's manuals, etc. (Preda 2009). Roy Stager Jacques (1996) has traced the genealogy of management knowledge in the US from the nineteenth to the twenty-first century, mixing a Foucauldian inspired analysis of shifting discourse and knowledge regimes with labour history. Giorgio Agamben (2011) seeks to describe the genealogy of economy, political governance, and power.

One "genre" which is often genealogical in its approach may be said to revolve around "*moral economy*," that is, it concerns the *legitimacy* of past economic (social, political) arrangements and quarrels or struggles concerning this legitimacy. Some studies of economic intellectual history are particularly interested in questions concerning legitimacy, posing questions such as: how has capitalism been justified (or criticized)? How has poverty and inequality

---

18 Again, I am much indebted to Thorup (2012) for this way of categorizing different methodologies or genres of intellectual history.

been discussed? How was slavery justified? Economic systems and economic relationships have throughout most of Western history been addressed in a moral discourse, i.e. dealing with questions of legitimacy. A few examples may serve to illustrate this. Jon D. Wisman and James F. Smith (2011) demonstrate how inequality has been justified in the past as well as today (mainly in the US), especially looking at the role various religions as well as different economic theories in each their different way have promoted arguments that justified inequality. In his classic book of 1977, Albert O. Hirschman traces what he refers to as *political* arguments for "capitalism" before its triumph. Central to his thesis is that the "cool" and "rational" interests were called upon to *counter* the "dangerous passions" that constantly led European states into war with one another, and that the rise of a "modern economy" would discipline political rulers. It can also be called a "history of legitimization," because its central aim is to show how "capitalism" was justified in its early stages.

As noted in the above, studies of economic intellectual history have not only been made by intellectual historians. Economic sociology has contributed with many studies concerning legitimization and criticism of capitalism, cf,. e.g., Luc Boltanski and Eve Chiapello (2005). A central question posed here is, again, how capitalism as an economic system was justified (and criticized) in different times and spaces. Intellectual historian Quentin Skinner (2002) has also written about the legitimization of economic action, which could be subsumed under the heading of this "history of legitimization." Histories of legitimization ask different kinds of questions than history of economic thought. There is a large difference between the interest in e.g. the development of economic theory in relation to the theory of money or discussions of macroeconomic policy, to questions related to the legitimacy of economic systems and relationships. A history of legitimization would typically involve historical reconstruction (but could also consist of analytical reconstruction, e.g. demonstrating the reoccurrence of the "same" argument for poverty in the public debate, although historical context should be taken into account). It is more adequate to subsume "history of legitimization" under the heading of economic intellectual history, than under the heading of "history of economic thought," as the first is not confined to studying the development of economic theory.

Conceptual history seems to be finding its way into economic intellectual history, i.e., as the study of the history of economic concepts. Whereas some studies are clearly influenced by Reinhart Koselleck or other main contributors to the discipline of conceptual history, other histories of concepts exist which do not seem to be affiliated with the work of Koselleck or other related conceptual historians.[19] *Historical contextualism* (e.g., "the Cambridge School"), may also be said to have worked with the history of political economy, as also seen in some of the above mentioned work by Quentin Skinner and J. G. A. Pocock, although the history of political thought has been the schools' primary concern. *Science studies* or the history of economic science, has used methods of economic sociology and of intellectual history to move outside the narrower boundaries of "the history of economic thought," often embracing a more "constructivist" perspective on the history of economics.[20] The work of "heterodox" economists such as Philip Mirowski, for instance, has attracted much attention. In Mirowski's (1989) *More Heat Than Light: Economics as Social Physics, Physics as Nature's Economics*, he investigates the rise of neo-classical economics and the "marginal revolution" in the 1870s. Mirowski's basic claim is that neo-classical economics was reshaping the science of economics by using physics as its scientific ideal. By rigorously applying mathematics, by formalising economic relationships, and by trying to develop a "pure" science, economics would be able to abstract from historical context. Thermodynamics and the idea of a "general equilibrium" were instrumental for the way in which neo-classical economists conceptualized the economy. Mirowski's historical reconstruction is a reconstruction of how neo-classical economics developed as a science, questioning its epistemology and its modelling of the world by placing and conditioning its rise in the intellectual historical context of late nineteenth century physics. It destabilizes the foundations of neo-classical economics by bringing attention to the historical and intellectual contingency of its rise.[21] *Cultural historical intellectual history* or *deconstructivism/*

19 For examples of research that relies upon Koselleck's work, see, e.g., Klaes (2001); Klaes and Sent (2005). For examples of "conceptual histories" with little or no affiliation with the German discipline of conceptual history, see e.g. Elkjær (1991); Mitchell (1998); Murphy, Liao and Welsch (2006).

20 Cf., e.g., Poovey (1998) for a compelling account of "the fact," especially numbers and numerical representations of facts, in which Poovey, mainly relying upon a Foucauldian approach, traces the history of double-entry bookkeeping, and the sciences of wealth and society (economics and social science) and their epistemological usage of especially numbers as facts.

21 Blaug (2001, 161) also acknowledges Mirowski's work, labelling it as "what the Germans used to call *Geistesgeschichte*," referring to the shift from a perspective centred on individual key actors (economic thinkers) towards a perspective which looks at general developments in society's discourse, science, etc. According to Blaug, this work offers "a style of history in which we care less what the great minds of the past actually said and care more about the intellectual milieu in which they said it" (Blaug 2001, 161). Another prominent example of a "contingency view" on economic science comparable to Mirowski's, is Marion Fourcade's (2009) *Economists and Societies. Discipline and Profession in the United States, Britain, and France, 1890s to 1990s*. Fourcade's sociological work traces the comparative development of the economist profession in the US, Britain, and France, with different public roles, different ideas, methodologies, self-perceptions, economic knowledge, etc. being "produced"

literary intellectual history can also be found which deals specifically with economic intellectual history. Jean-Joseph Goux's (1994) *The Coiners of Language*,
for instance, looks at the parallel histories of the end of realism in the novel
and the end of gold money in the late nineteenth century. It asks whether "it
[was] purely by chance that the crisis of realism in the novel and in paint-
ing coincided with the end of gold money?" Ian Baucam's (2005) *Specters of
the Atlantic: Finance Capital, Slavery, and the Philosophy of History*, for instance,
blends together literary theory, philosophy, and social science in a history of
the trans-Atlantic slave trade. Finally, history of mentality or "spirit" and the
French Annales School was from its very beginning preoccupied with economic "intellectual" history (Braudel 1985).

Examples of "Historical Reconstructions" of Economic (Social and Political) Thought

In the previous section we saw that, if we adapt a broader view of economic
intellectual history, we can find examples of work within different branches
of intellectual history. We can also see that interesting work has been written
by people who do not identify themselves as intellectual historians, but whose
work is highly relevant for the further development of economic intellectual
history. And we have seen that, apart from the already established genres of
intellectual history, we should note than one genre of economic intellectual
history is particularly concerned with histories of legitimization (or what we
might call "historical moral economy").

As one genre has been described as "rational reconstructions" of the history
of economic thought, another (broad) category is "historical" reconstructions. In this section, we take a closer look at the somewhat abstract category
of historical reconstruction, in order to draw in further examples of research,
and to try to develop further categorizations of economic intellectual history.

The distinction between rational reconstructions and historical reconstructions is a distinction running cross the different genres of intellectual
history mentioned above (that is, a work can be history of science and historical reconstruction at the same time). If we again take the second step in
expanding the scope and interests of economic intellectual history, we can
move from economic science more narrowly to social and political thought,
which is often intertwined with economic thinking. Historical reconstructions of economic theory pose different kinds of questions than analytical

---

nationally. Her work thereby questions the idea of an alleged universality of economics. Cf. also the
review symposium discussing Fourcade's work in (Gazier, Hall and Hodgson 2010, 747–64).

reconstructions. A few examples will serve to illustrate this point. Chiapello's (2007) article on accounting and the birth of the notion of capitalism, starts with noticing how the relationship between the rise of rational accounting practices, especially double-entry bookkeeping (debit and credit), and the rise of capitalism, has been discussed since classical sociologists such as Max Weber and Werner Sombart. Chiapello thus shifts the attention from the historical link between accounting and capitalism to the intellectual domain, arguing that accounting (double entry bookkeeping) played a key role for the way in which Marx came to understand capital and its ability to accumulate and to abstract from the concrete materializations of goods and of liquidity (money). Chiapello historically reconstructs one context of the development of Marx's thought. The question is not whether Marx was right or wrong, or how he influenced economic theory, but what influenced his way of thinking about capitalism. And the thesis is that the historical practice of double entry bookkeeping was nothing but crucial to the development of his theory of capital. Emma Rothschild's (2001) book on Adam Smith attempts a historical reconstruction of Adam Smith's thoughts in the context of the enlightenment and of moral philosophy. What matters in this kind of economic intellectual history is not so much how Adam Smith contributed to economic theory, but how we could understand the broader scope and ambitions of his intellectual project.[22] Again, there is a broadening of the scope of interest as compared to analytical reconstructions of economic thought. Jerry Z. Muller's (2003) *The Mind and the Market: Capitalism in Modern European Thought* on key thinkers in the West who either justified or critiqued the rise of industrial capitalism, again illustrates a shift from a more "narrow" preoccupation with the history of economic thought, to a view which focuses upon economic ideas and arguments in a "broader" sense. Instead of asking who contributed to economic theory, the question raised here concerns who were the influential intellectuals that responded to the rise of industrial capitalism. This is not simply history of economic theory, but an intellectual history of capitalism in the context of social and political thought. Once we move outside the attempt to make rational reconstructions of economic theory, the area of interest also becomes broader. Not confined to the development of economic theory as theory, there is a shift of attention towards what I have loosely called economic ideas and arguments (such as debates on poverty, for instance, or on the nature of different economic systems), which may fall outside the scope of

---

22 Again, it should be noted that such an endeavour goes back to at least Donald Winch (1978).

contributions to economic theory, narrowly understood, but still be central to economic and political discussions.

More generally, we may note that an important genre of historical reconstruction which contributes to economic intellectual history emerges by looking at the trajectory of economic thought in relation to political and social thought, and often to social history, in specified historical contexts. This may be seen in the works of, e.g., Rothschild (2001) and Winch (1978). Topics are political economy in the aftermath of the English industrial revolution, American nineteenth century political economic thought, American twentieth-century economic and political thought, economic thinking in the Middle Ages, etc.[23] This genre may again be contrasted to traditional histories of economic thought, interested in economic ideas and arguments in the broader context of social and political thought, and sometimes in the social and political context as well. How did previous times' cultures and historical actors make sense of the world they lived in—a world which was also "economic?" How did society's discourse about economic matters, political economy, markets, value, money, etc., change over time? It is a genre which often traces what could be called "big shifts" in social discourse. Three monographs in American history serve as examples of this genre. In Howard Brick's (2006) *Transcending Capitalism: Visions of a New Society in Modern American Thought*, Brick demonstrates how, in the period from around World War I until the 1970s, there was a broad current of thought in America, across much of the political spectrum, which thought that American society was moving towards a new economic system. There was what Brick refers to as a "post-capitalist" vision, shared by many intellectuals on both the left and the right. In a word, the idea that America had moved, or was in the process of developing into something decisively different than "capitalism" (namely a welfare state or a bureaucratic, industrial society, etc.), was something around which

---

23 There is, of course, a vast amount of such books in the genre of economic intellectual history which have clearly defined temporal and spatial boundaries, and which do not look at the analytical development of economics as a science. To list just a few examples: A. M. C. Waterman (1991) demonstrates the continuing role played by religion in the development of classical political economy, which again illustrates the point made here about an economic intellectual history which looks at economic ideas in their broader historical and intellectual context, not in the context of the (cumulative) development of economics as a science. Lianna Farber (2006) offers a new account of the view on trade in the Middle Ages, using a variety of literary, theological, and legal sources. Maxine Berg (1980) looks at the rise of political economy in the context of debates about industrialization and machinery. Anna Gambles (1999) traces nineteenth-century conservative economic thinking as distinct and being in opposition to free trade liberalism, a work which is also self-consciously marked as a different approach than "'doctrinal accounts' of the development of formal economic thought" (Gambles 1999, 2).

there was some degree of consensus. And the aim of Brick's book is to demonstrate the history of this "vision," and the break with it in the 1970s. A similar ambition can be found in Jeffrey Sklansky's (2002) *The Soul's Economy: Market Society and Selfhood in American Thought, 1820–1920*, where Sklansky traces the rise of a new understanding of the market society and the individual's role in it around 1900. This "social self" which developed in the context of industrial capitalism marked a fundamental break with earlier republican ideals of self-ownership and self-rule. A third example is aforementioned Daniel Rodgers's *Age of Fracture* (2011), which traces another major shift in society's self-understanding, this time from the post-war period until today's "age of fracture." This "genre" is more interested in what mattered in the public debate and about what was said by influential intellectuals and other public speakers concerning the nature and quality of our economic world, than in what happened at the desk of economists. As we shall see in the next section, however, in contrast to the "new history of economic thought," it remains more "traditional" in at least two ways. First, authors such as Brick obviously recognize global or transnational history, and emphasize e.g. the way in which US intellectual history has continuously been influenced by European thought. But these books are first and foremost books on US intellectual history. Second, whereas new history of economic thought deliberately seeks to expand the terrain from "high" to "medium" and "low" levels of actors and historical sources, this genre primarily sticks to the more familiar sources of intellectual history, i.e., important works by intellectuals and other public figures of various kinds. To summarize: this genre sees economic ideas and arguments in the broader context of society's discourse; it sticks to a national context but is aware of the "transnational turn," and it mainly relies upon classical sources of intellectual history.[24]

A "New History of Economic Thought"

As seen in the above sections, there is already much work within the discipline of intellectual history and other disciplines which contribute to the genre of economic intellectual history, and which differs markedly from the bulk of "traditional" history of economic thought. Towards the end of this article, we will take a closer look at the self-consciously oppositional concept of a "new history of economic thought." This will be useful for further conceptual discussion of what economic intellectual history is—also if it wants to preserve

---

24 Rodgers, however, also includes e.g., political speeches, economics textbooks, and a variety of other sources.

some autonomy as a particular discipline dissimilar to, e.g., "history" or "history of economic life."

"New History of Economic Thought" is connected to the research project Exchanges of Economic, Legal and Political Ideas, located at the Centre for History and Economics at Cambridge and Harvard.[25] The new history of economic thought seems to be leaning towards historical reconstructions rather than rational reconstructions. It seeks, however, to move beyond the history of economic theory and thought, towards a history of economic *life*. Three features of this project deserve to be mentioned. First, the project aims at a *broad contextualization* of economic and political thinking within the context of economic, religious and legal history, taking its starting place around 1750. Second, the project has a distinct *transnational* scope—indeed, this new history of economic thought seeks to bring the field of economic intellectual history in alignment with the transnational or global turn. Third, it moves beyond the traditional economic thought's preoccupation with "high" or scientific thought, moving towards a "medium" level of economic thought, i.e., publicists, public bureaucrats, entrepreneurs, participants in the public debate, and so forth. Debates about free trade versus protectionism, or issues related to migration or the empires' political economy, often took place at this level, and not (or not only) at the level of "high" scientific discourse. This "new history of economic thought" even incorporates a third layer, a "low" level of economic thought, trying to trace the history of the economic life of laymen, slaves, etc., often through legal documents. It is not too surprising, then, that it is also referred to as a new history of economic life, since it deliberately moves beyond the "intellectual realm" of economic theory, thought, ideas and arguments, towards this level of describing the economic life of different groups, classes and individuals. Indeed, an aim of this project is to give rebirth to an economic-*cultural* history. In summary, this "new history of economic thought" distinguishes itself from traditional history of economic thought. It contextualizes economic thought broadly; it moves beyond "high" to "medium" and "low" levels of economic thought; and it embraces the global turn wholeheartedly.

By including the "low" level of economic thought, trying to capture the

---

25 The following refers to the descriptions of "new history of economic thought" at the website. See the programmes' website for further information (http://www.fas.harvard.edu/~histecon/exel/). Readers interested in recent research networks working with economic intellectual history may also want to visit, e.g., the "culture of the market" group to be found at http://www.arts.manchester.ac.uk/cultureofthemarket/, or the "history of economic rationality" group to be found here: http://ecora.au.dk/.

"economic life" of the past, however, it also seems to move *beyond* traditional boundaries of *intellectual* history into what economic historian William H. Sewell, Jr. quoted at the beginning of this article refers to as "history of economic life." This "new history of economic thought" self-consciously blurs the distinction between *intellectual* history and history (of economic life). In relation to the present context of exploring ways in which intellectual historians can study economic intellectual history, it seems that there might be some risk involved here. That is, if we are interested in preserving some autonomy of *intellectual* history, as something distinct from (other branches of) history. First, we may note that if the term "intellectual" is perhaps stretched so that it does not refer only to the study of intellectuals, but instead to intellectual (cognitive and linguistic) *activity*, we may appreciate that thinking, theory-building, etc., is not something which is unique for intellectuals, but common to human beings as such.[26] This supports studying not only "high" levels, but also "medium" and "low" levels. Forgotten and "left out" voices, marginalized groups, etc., will finally be heard, as has been one key feature of social history. If economic intellectual history is to do this, however, it might be suggested that it chooses particularly to focus upon discourse, text, giving meaning to economic life, etc., and not to e.g. writing the histories of social classes. One task again, then, if we want to preserve intellectual history as being something unique, remains in not erasing all boundaries between intellectual and social history, while building constructively on the latter.

Conclusion

Whereas this article is not an attempt at a full review of research on the history of economic ideas and argumentation, it has mapped key approaches from both outside as well as from inside the discipline of intellectual history. What has been referred to as "economic intellectual history" has been a part of intellectual history since at least the 1970s, as can be witnessed from the substantive scholarship on for example Adam Smith, see again Rothschild (2001) or Winch (1978). But intellectual historians have, to say the least, not been alone in writing the history of economic thinking. The "history of economic thought" is a well-established genre, and often with economists as contributors, highlighting the development of economic theory. Since

---

26 Philosophically, such an argument could be defended by e.g. different forms of pragmatism which seek to undermine the distinction between "high level" thinking and theorizing done at universities, as opposed to "low level" thinking and theorizing by mere "practitioners" and lay people (see for example Dewey (1910) or Schön (1983)). Another branch of pragmatism, pragmatic sociology, has argued for the equal distribution of critical capacity of people. Cf. Boltanski and Thévenot (1999).

intellectual history has recently broadened its scope (methodology, research objects, actors, etc.), however, this broadening of scope has also been (and can become even more) reflected in new histories of economic ideas, thought, argumentation, discourse, etc. Intellectual history has alternative historical perspectives to offer than "history of economic thought" mostly written by economists with historical interests, and typically concerned with what Joseph Schumpeter referred to as the "history of economic analysis." Indeed, an important premise for further development of economic intellectual history is to continue to look beyond the more narrow interest in the thought of key (political) economists. This is not to dismiss either traditional history of economic thought or the important contextualizing and constructivist histories of economics. Rather, the point is to highlight that there are also other, interesting options. Secondly, intellectual history can learn from and build upon other contemporary historical studies of economic discourse and ideas found in, e.g., economic sociology and histories or genealogies of economic discourse. To this we could count, for instance, analysis of discourse and of genealogies as by those following in footsteps of Michel Foucault. Another example is economic sociology and the idea of the "performativity of economics," that is, how economic technologies and ideas "do not just describe the world, but are profoundly involved in shaping it" through the very way in which it models the world (Fourcade and Healy 2007, 302).[27] Viviana A. Zelizer's work (e.g. 2011) on the social meaning of money, and more generally on the historical and cultural contingencies of economic subjects, might also be a source of inspiration for economic intellectual history. Such theoretical developments are interesting from the point of view of economic intellectual history because they highlight the role of ideas. These and other studies, from e.g. anthropology, philosophy, etc., are of much relevance for intellectual history, that is, if it wants to engage even more with the history of economic ideas and argumentation, and if intellectual history is conceived in broader terms than traditionally has been the case.

Finally, I will briefly sketch the present state (and maybe even future development) of economic intellectual history. I have argued that such an economic intellectual history can be global, national, or local. It can contextualize the history of economic thought, broadly conceived, and show how economic discourse develops in the context of, e.g., other sciences, religious, political or moral discourse, in a particular intellectual context. Indeed, this

---

27 For original articulations of the idea of the "performativity of economics," see, e.g., Callon (1998) or Caliskan and Callon (2009).

has been a key contribution of economic intellectual history since its very beginning, as can be seen in, e.g., the revisionist scholarship on Adam Smith. Economic intellectual history can investigate classical sources and 'high level' actors, such as public intellectuals, political economists, etc., and continue to enrich our understanding of Marx, Smith, or Keynes. But it can also study "medium" level actors who produce government statements, think tank policy recommendations, international economic organization reports, popular management and business books, business and labour organization documents, stock market investors' manuals, etc. And it might even study "low level" actors, whether they are slaves, housewives, peasants, students, traders, etc. While connecting to or building upon work from other disciplines such as social history, history of capitalism, economic history, etc., however, it might be suggested that the focus of economic *intellectual* history remains the production, spread, absorption, sense-making of economic reasoning, knowledge, meaning, discourse, metaphors, etc.[28] By "economic," it refers not just to economic theory and to the work of economists, but to a host of subjects such as money, value, finance, business, management, labour, and so on. It does not forget that the very term "economic" should be treated with precaution, however, as economic discourse often is inseparable from political and moral discourse. The study of economic ideas, discourse, and thinking does *not* imply that these are, *eo ipso*, only economic matters. Furthermore, it is aware of the historical contingencies involved in the production of economic knowledge and reasoning (and their critiques), as well as how the meaning attached to concepts such as freedom, property, debt, work, labour, the corporation, unemployment, the market, shift through time—this often as results of ideological battles around defining our moral, economic, social, and political languages. It can draw upon a variety of methodologies such as conceptual history, genealogy, linguistic pragmatism, science studies, cultural intellectual history, history of mentalities. It may be interested more in, e.g., moral economy than the development of economics as a science, asking questions about how slavery, wage labour, exploitation, taxation, poverty, protectionism, etc., was legitimized at different points in time. It may inquire into what role economics played in this respect. And it takes recent developments outside of intellectual history, as, e.g., economic sociology, under careful consideration, as they can contribute to a further enrichment of economic intellectual history. Such an economic intellectual history may also be able

---

28 On the role of metaphors in economic theory and reasoning, see, e.g., McCloskey (1985, 1990, 2000).

to perform what Reinhart Koselleck once called a "semantic control" of our economic vocabulary. It may inquire into the metaphors, concepts, interpretations, etc., in historical or contemporary use around, e.g., "financial crisis," debt, unemployment, economic freedom, and taxation. It may inquire into the ways in which particular forms of economic reasoning are legitimized, or which moral and normative resources it draws upon. And it does not forget the "politics of language," and that a central way in which power is manifest is through the very right to define and interpret our world, to be the speaker of truth, and hold the key to authoritative knowledge.

References

Agamben, G. 2011. *The Kingdom and the Glory.* Stanford: Stanford University Press.

Backhouse, R. E. 2008. Review of *History of Economic Thought as an Intellectual Discipline,* by D. P. O'Brien, *Economic History Review* 61, no. 2: 741–42.

Barber, W. J. 2007. Review of *The Wealth of Ideas: A History of Economic Thought,* by Alessandro Roncaglia, *History of Political Economy* 39, no. 3: 551–52.

Barma, N. H., and S. K. Vogel, eds. 2008. *Political Economy Reader: Markets as Institutions.* New York: Routledge.

Baucom, I. 2005. *Specters of the Atlantic: Finance Capital, Slavery, and the Philosophy of History.* Durham, NC: Duke University Press.

Bavaj, R. 2010. "Intellectual History." *Docupedia*-Zeitgeschicte. Accessed September 13, 2012. https://docupedia.de/zg/Intellectual_History?oldid=76819.

Becker, C. 2008. "Thoreau's Economic Philosophy." *European Journal of the History of Economic Thought* 15, no. 2: 211–46.

Berg, M. 1980. *The Machinery Question and the Making of Political Economy, 1815-1848.* Cambridge: Cambridge University Press.

Blaug, M. 1997. *Economic Theory in Retrospect.* Cambridge: Cambridge University Press.

———. 2001. "No History of Ideas, Please, We're Economists." *Journal of Economic Perspectives* 15, no. 1: 145–64.

Boltanski, L., and É. Chiapello2005. *The New Spirit of Capitalism.* London: Verso.

Boltanski, L., and L. Thévenot. 1999. "The Sociology of Critical Capacity." *European Journal of Social Theory* 2, no. 3: 359–78.

Braudel, F. 1985. *Civilization and Capitalism, 15th–18th Century.* 3 vols. London: Fontana.

Brick, H. 2006. *Transcending Capitalism: Visions of a New Society in Modern American Thought.* Ithaca, NY: Cornell University Press.

Caliskan, K., and M. Callon. 2009. "Economization, Part 1: Shifting Attention from the Economy towards Processes of Economization." *Economy and Society* 38, no. 3: 369–98.

Callon, M. 1998. "Introduction: The Embeddedness of Economic Markets in Economics." In *The Laws of the Markets,* edited by Michel Callon, 1–57. Oxford: Blackwell.

Chiapello, È. 2007. "Accounting and the Birth of the Notion of Capitalism." *Critical Perspectives on Accounting* 18: 263–93.

Collini, S. 2012. "Intellectual History." Assessed October 3, 2012. http://www.history.ac.uk/makinghistory/resources/articles/intellectual_history.html.

De Goede, M. 2005. *A Genealogy of Finance: Virtue, Fortune, and Faith*. Minneapolis: University of Minnesota Press.

Dewey, J. 1910. *How We Think*. Boston: D.C. Heath & Co. Publishers.

Elkjær, J. R. 1991. "The Entrepreneur in Economic Theory: An Example of the Development and Influence of a Concept." *History of European Ideas* 13, no. 6: 805–15.

Farber, L. 2006. *An Anatomy of Trade in Medieval Writing: Value, Consent, and Community*. Ithaca, NY: Cornell University Press.

Fourcade, M. 2009. *Economists and Societies: Discipline and Profession in the United States, Britain, and France, 1890s to 1990s*. Cambridge: Cambridge University Press.

Fourcade, M., and K. Healy. 2007. "Moral Views of Market Society." *Annual Review of Sociology* 33: 285–311.

Galbraith, J. K. 1987. *A History of Economics: The Past as the Present*. London: Hamish Hamilton.

Gambles, A. 1999. *Protection and Politics: Conservative Economic Discourse, 1815–1852*. Woodbridge: The Boydell Press.

Gazier, B., P. A. Hall and G. M. Hodgson. 2010. Review of Marion Fourcade, *Economists and Societies: Discipline and Profession in the United States, Britain and France. Socio-Economic Review* 8, no. 4: 747–64.

Gordon, P. E. 2012. "What Is Intellectual History? A Frankly Partisan Introduction to a Frequently Misunderstood Field." Assessed October 3, 2012. http://history.fas.harvard.edu/people/faculty/documents/pgordon-whatisintellhist.pdf.

Goux, J.-J. 1994. *The Coiners of Language*. Translated by Jennifer Curtiss Gage. Norman: University of Oklahoma Press.

Gregory, C. 2009. "Whatever Happened to Economic Anthropology?" *The Australian Journal of Anthropology* 20: 285–300.

Heilbroner, R. L. 1953. *The Worldly Philosophers: The Lives, Times and Ideas of the Great Economic Thinkers*. New York: Simon & Schuster.

Hirschman, A. O. 1977. *The Passions and the Interests: Political Arguments for Capitalism before Its Triumph*. Princeton: Princeton University Press.

Jacques, R. S. 1996. *Manufacturing the Employee: Management Knowledge from the 19th to the 21th Centuries*. London: Sage.

Klaes, M. 2001. "Begriffsgeshichte: Between the Scylla of Conceptual and the Charybdis of Institutional History of Economics." *Journal of the History of Economic Thought* 23, no. 2: 153–79.

Klaes, M., and Sent, E.-M. 2005. "A Conceptual History of the Emergence of Bounded Rationality." *History of Political Economy* 37, no. 1: 28–59.

Marx, K. 1990. *Capital*, 3 volumes. London: Penguin Books.

McCloskey, D. N. 1989. *The Rhetoric of Economics*. Brighton: Wheatsheaf.

————. 1990. *If You're So Smart: The Narrative of Economic Expertise*. Chicago: University of Chicago Press.

————. 1994. *Knowledge and Persuasion in Economics*. Cambridge: Cambridge University Press.

Michaelides, P., O. Kardasi, and J. Milios 2011. "Democritus's Economic Ideas in the Context of Classical Political Economy." *European Journal of the History of Economic Thought* 18, no. 1: 1–18.

Mirowski, P. 1989. *More Heat Than Light: Economics as Social Physics, Physics as Nature's Economics*. Cambridge: Cambridge University Press.

Mitchell, T. 1998. "Fixing the Economy." *Cultural Studies* 12, no. 1: 82–101.

Morley, N. 1998. "Political Economy and Classical Antiquity." *Journal of the History of Ideas* 59, no. 1: 95–114.

Muller, J. Z. 2003. *The Mind and the Market: Capitalism in Modern European Thought*. New York: Anchor Books.

Murphy, P. J., J. Liao and H.P. Welsch 2006. "A Conceptual History of Entrepreneurial Thought." *Journal of Management History* 1, no. 12: 12–35.

O'Brien, D. P. 2007 *History of Economic Thought as an Intellectual Discipline*. Cheltenham and Northampton, MA: Edward Elgar.

Perlman, M., and C. R. McCann 2000. *The Pillars of Economic Understanding*. 2 vols. Ann Arbor, Michigan: University of Michigan Press.

Pocock, J. G. A. 1985. *Virtue, Commerce, and History: Essays on Political Thought: Chiefly in the Eighteenth Century*. Cambridge: Cambridge University Press.

Poovey, M. 1998. *A History of the Modern Fact: Problems of Knowledge in the Sciences of Wealth and Society*. Cambridge: Cambridge University Press.

Preda, A. 2009. *Framing Finance: The Boundaries of Markets and Modern Capitalism*. Chicago: University of Chicago Press.

Ricardo, D. 2004. *The Principles of Political Economy and Taxation*. Mineola: Dover Publications.

Rodgers, D. T. 2011. *Age of Fracture*. Cambridge, MA: The Belknap Press of Harvard University Press

Roncaglia, A. 2006. *The Wealth of Ideas: A History of Economic Thought*. Cambridge, Cambridge University Press.

Rorty, R. 1984. "The Historiography of Philosophy: Four Genres." In *Philosophy in History: Essays on the Historiography of Philosophy*, edited by Richard Rorty, J. B. Schneewind, and Quentin Skinner, 49–75. Cambridge: Cambridge University Press.

Rothbard, M. 1995. *Economic Thought before Adam Smith and Classical Economics.* 2 vols. Aldershot: Edward Elgar Publishing.

Rothschild, E. 2001. *Economic Sentiments: Adam Smith, Concordet and the Enlightenment.* Cambridge, MA: Harvard University Press.

Sandelin, B., H.-M. Trautwein, and R. Wundrak 2008. *A Short History of Economic Thought.* London: Routledge.

Schön, D. A. 1983. *The Reflective Practitioner: How Professionals Think in Action.* New York: Basic Books.

Schumpeter, J. A. 1954. *History of Economic Analysis.* Oxford: Oxford University Press.

Sewell, W. H. Jr. 2010. "A Strange Career: The Historical Study of Economic Life." *History and Theory* 49: 146–66.

Sklansky, J. 2002. *The Soul's Economy: Market Society and Selfhood in American Thought, 1820–1920.* Chapell Hill: University of North Carolina Press.

———. 2012. "The Elusive Sovereign: New Intellectual and Social Histories of Capitalism." *Modern Intellectual History* 9, no. 1: 233–48.

Skinner, Q. 2002. *Visions of Politics,* vol. 1. Cambridge, MA: Cambridge University Press.

Smith, A. 2009. *The Wealth of Nations.* Hampshire: Harriman House.

Teichgraeber, R. F. 2004. "Capitalism and Intellectual History." *Modern Intellectual History* 1, no. 2: 267–82.

Thorup, M. 2012. "Intellektuel Historie." *Temp* 4: 177–89.

Walter, R. 2008. "The Economy and Pocock's Political Economy." *History of European Ideas* 34: 334–44.

Waterman, A. M. C. 1991. *Revolution, Economics, and Religion: Christian Political Economy 1798–1833.* Cambridge, MA: Cambridge University Press.

Winch, D. 1978. *Adam Smith's Politics: An Essay in Historiographic Revision.* Cambridge: Cambridge University Press.

———. 1996. *Riches and Poverty: An Intellectual History of Political Economy in Britain, 1750–1834.* New York: Cambridge University Press.

Wisman, J. D., and J. F. Smith 2011. "Legitimating Inequality: Fooling Most of the People Most of the Time." *The American Journal of Economics and Sociology* 70, no. 4: 974–1014.

Zelizer, V. A. 2011. *Economic Lives: How Culture shapes the Economy.* Princeton: Princeton University Press.

Perfect Liberty or Natural Liberty?
Adam Smith, François Quesnay and the Problem of Ordering Eighteenth Century Economies

Stefan Gaardsman Jacobsen[1]

The article investigates the concept of natural order as it is used by François Quesnay and Adam Smith in their respective economic writings. While Smith used the concept only after having visited Quesnay and the Physiocrats in France in the 1760s, in *The Wealth of Nations* he sought to negotiate the meaning of what was "natural" about economic life. The Physiocrats believed it possible to identify a model or a perfect regime of natural order—an order that they in fact thought to exist and function in China due to a rigorous system of economic laws. Smith sided with contemporary critics of this metaphysical vision of economic perfection (and of Chinese governance), but he suggested that the economic mechanisms of the physiocratic theories would remain intact even with a minimum of control by state laws. However, Smith's balancing act on these questions remained disputed even by his Scottish successors in political economy, and the problem of ordering the society from the vantage point of an economic science was rephrased as a problem of combining the physiocratic metaphysics of natural order with the "business of the world" as expounded by Smith.

The Contexts of Economic Order

The continuity of economics as an over three hundred year old scientific tradition is a strong narrative in the history of economic thought. Although "economics" is no longer posited as a Lovejoyean "unit idea" improved brick by brick over this period, certain theoretical components are seen as having sustained their truth value or their authority through centuries (Coleman 2002). Still, excluding the debates of eighteenth century historians, contemporary interest in Adam Smith and the Physiocrats is prompted by their image as progressive economists (see, e.g., Gwartney 2009, 4; Fry 1992). Thus, their historical roles as eighteenth-century interpreters of classical literature, moral law, metaphysics or epistemology are faded in favor of their "prophetic"

1 Stefan Gaardsmand Jacobsen is assistant professor in the Department of Culture and Society, Program for Philosophy and History of Ideas, Aarhus University.

insights into the workings of economic systems. An example of a specific theoretical component often taken to designate the originality of Smithian economics is the concept of spontaneous order. In fact, Smith never used this concept and it was first developed as part of a coherent economic theory by Austrian economist Friedrich Hayek in the 1960s. In the twentieth century context, spontaneity was addressed via principles of evolutionary biology. For Hayek this was central, as he sought to avoid any metaphysical assumptions at the core of his economic theories (Hayek 1978, 253ff.). However, since the latter part of the twentieth century, historians of economic thought have continuously attempted to prove a historical end epistemological connection between Hayek's theories and classical economic thought, especially by claiming that the concept of the invisible hand in Adam Smith can be interpreted as the idea of spontaneous order "in spe" (see, e.g., Petsoulas 2001; Hamowy 1987; Young 2008; Smith 2006). Although Smith never used the concept of spontaneous order, the assumed historical presence of this notion supports a narrative of scientific qualities of economics that has presumable been sustained since the eighteenth century.

This article focuses on eighteenth century writings and specifically on Adam Smith's and the Physiocrats' own ambitions to formulate a theory of societal order grounded in political economy. The claims to a scientific basis of economics were not uncommon in this age, but the meanings of claims to science differ in fundamental ways from conceptions born in the nineteenth and twentieth centuries. For most proponents of the Scottish enlightenment, and for the dominating French voices on political economy in the period, no arguments for an emergent economic order which were expected to deliver predictable and scientifically testable results. Rather, the positive outcomes were not "the effect of any human wisdom," as Smith would put it, had to rely on theologically informed notions of order (Smith 1976 [1776], i, 17). Rather than as a spontaneous order, this principle was formulated as a "natural order" that built on a long tradition of translating Christian theological discourse into a political and commercial realm. Thus, against the narrative of a sustain tradition of spontaneous order, the contextual analyses of this article show that Smith's conceptual innovations were a conceptual negotiation of contemporary political beliefs that had not abandoned the metaphysical traditions. Moreover, by taking a detailed look at how these traditions were negotiated in new economic theories, this article documents how universalist ideas made it relevant for economists not just to relate to European economies, but also to systems attributed to the Chinese Empire.

Although many, if not most, of the Smithian and physiocratic insights have been questioned either theoretically or empirically, there is still a tendency to acknowledge the originality of their thinking about an economic *system* in which different producing, consuming and trading activities were interconnected. What seems to point ahead and to be the forerunner of any modern (macro-)economic theory, is that the understanding of the system allows us to make connections between the rights and wrongs in specific practices in terms of whether they promote national wealth or not (see, e.g., Skinner 1996, 128). The early descriptions of economic systems were not purely descriptive and this is where the concept of order became relevant for these late eighteenth century thinkers. Smith and the Physiocrats, along with several other writers of their time, were deeply concerned for the future outlook of their respective state economies. The systematizing efforts on a conceptual level were also attempts at establishing consensus around a specific political order of society; creating and upholding the right policies for the state.

While there is not much doubt in the literature that the concept of natural order, as it was used until the early eighteenth century, carried heavy theological implications (Reill 2005, 37; Porter 2003, 744), it remains more unclear how it was renegotiated by later eighteenth century political theorists. In a recent article, Jeffrey T. Young has made a complete narrative of a specifically protestant tradition of natural law gradually becoming operational for economics through the works Pufendorf, Francis Hutcheson and Adam Smith (Young 2008).[2] While this analysis seem to have some merit, it is interesting that Young does not account for the concept of *natural order*, but remains focused on a narrower definition of *natural law*. If one takes a closer look at Smith's own vocabulary, the usage of "natural order" in his *The Wealth of Nations* (1776; WN) is in fact highly interesting, not least since the concept does *not* occur in his *Theory of Moral Sentiments* (TMS) from 1759 or in his *Lectures On Jurisprudence* from 1762–63. Therefore, in terms of philosophical premises, this concept can be seen as one of the important moves in the development of Smith's work from TMS to WN. In the period between the two works he paid visits to the workshop of French economist François Quesnay in Paris. Scottish political economist of a later generation than Smith, Francis Horner, wrote the following about the consequences of Smith's visit to France some fifty years before:

---

2 Andrew Skinner had made similar arguments in Skinner (1996, 109ff.).

That Smith did not precisely distinguish the real import of the economical system, is now confessed, we believe, even by those who agree with him in rejecting it. We are further satisfied that he derived a much larger portion of his reasonings from them, than he himself perhaps recollected; that his principles on the formation and distribution of riches approached more nearly to those of Quesnai, than he was himself aware... (Horner 1814, 447).

Horner was the student of Smith's student Dugald Stewart, and although the quote includes speculation as to Smith's recollection, it does suggest a much more central role for physiocratic thought than usually recognized in the literature on Smith's economic theories. Horner alludes to the principles of distribution and circulation, which are pivotal for the establishment of a sustainable economic order. Reviewing this and other nineteenth century conceptions, Andrew Skinner has conceded that "Smith evidently associated the thesis of the 'natural progress of opulence' with physiocratic teaching" (Skinner 1996, 138). However, Skinner has not unfolded in detail the background of the physiocratic beliefs and arguments about this "natural" component of the economic order, a component to which Smith was both attracted and repulsed.

Quesnay and his physiocratic movement have a prominent role in any account of the history of modern economic thought. Indeed, parallel to the scientific narrative on the idea of spontaneous order, the physiocratic theories are often referred to as the birth of modern economics (see e.g. Larrère 1992; Vaggi 1987; Meek 1963; Steiner 2003). As we shall see, the Physiocrats were certainly themselves convinced that they had invented a new science, though it was based on a highly abstract and metaphysically inspired epistemology. More specifically therefore, this article investigates how Smith understood the metaphysical principles contained in the physiocratic theories of natural order. Although this may seem as a very abstract problem, it subsequently had great import for the way in which Smith formulated his vision for economic governance. Smith was praiseful of the systematic understanding of the economy in the physiocratic writings, but he would not endorse the physiocratic belief that the whole economy could be scientifically predicted in detail. This meant a conflict between differing views on how to legislate: should the free mechanisms of the state's economy be forced through by few, but specific, rational maxims—as the Physiocrats would have it—or should there simply be as little governing as possible and let the "natural propensities" of the citizens lead to "natural liberty" and (hence) wealth in society?

These questions of the relation between economic life and governance where not invented by Smith and the Physiocrats. In fact, the conflict specifically echoes what Ian Hunter has called the "rival enlightenments" of voluntarism and rationalism in the seventeenth century (Hunter 2001). Here, two different understandings of natural law were developed in opposition to each other. One, suggested by rationalist as G. W. Leibniz and Christian Wolff, underlined the science of natural law as a possible path to understand and augment the perfection of all God's creations—including society and the state. Another, suggested by voluntarists as Samuel Pufendorf and Christian Thomasius, specifically limited the scope of natural law to *exclude* any course of action that relied on a sufficient human capability to improve or perfect society deliberately (Hunter 2003). Consequently, concepts like "liberty," "order" and any "naturalness" took on a very different meaning in the two respective camps, and I will point to the relevance of this philosophical background throughout the article. Conversely, as seen from Horner's words above, the conflict was not solved with Smith as the victorious voice for European political economy. Even Smith's own Scottish students were attracted to the metaphysical principles of order in the physiocratic vision.

The more immediate historical context in which one can understand the physiocratic innovations on the concept of natural order, is their reaction to Baron de Montesquieu's *The Spirit of the Laws*. Published in 1748, this was perhaps the most discussed work of the period, and it provoked the Physiocrats to develop a counter-theory of legislation to accompany their economic principles. This led them to oppose both Montesquieu's methodology generally and his specific analyses of different types of governance, as we shall see in the following section.[3]

Universality and the Laws

Montesquieu had set a new standard for arguing over political systems with his proto-sociological analyses of countries all over the (known) world in *The*

---

3 In the literature on the moral background to Smith's economic theories, the seminal theories by Albert O. Hirschmann have given the Mandevillian *Fable of the Bees* a central position (Hirschman 1977). My aim in this article is not to "write out" Mandeville of the history of eighteenth-century political economy, but my emphasis of my analyses goes in rather in the direction of highlighting certain continuities in moral thought than highlighting the discontinuities in religious thought Mandeville's fable certainly provoked.

Spirit of Laws in 1748 and its arguments were quickly acknowledged on the whole continent and in the British context (see, e.g., Oz-Salzberger 2003, 170). Although the reach and argumentative strength of the work was widely respected in the following decades, some were aggressively opposed to Montesquieu's analyses. Crudely put, Montesquieu had set the scene between a relativist and a universalist position on the question of government. Or, in more direct terms, the rift can be considered as the difference between a belief in one fundamental law that should underline a political constitution and the belief that a constitution should secure that power holders in society will "balance and check" each other. For rationalists writing in the natural law tradition, such as the Physiocrats, fundamental law was a moral code that had to be implemented in a precise way. The existence of such a fundamental law was a basic tenet that had been strengthening and expanding since the late seventeenth century. The respective camps of Leibnizians and Newtonians, known as fierce intellectual enemies on many scientific and epistemological subjects, shared a belief in the predictability of both physical and societal realms, often inferring the metaphor of a mechanism to explain the fundamental principle (Stollberg-Rilinger 1986, 28, 33, 153; Wootton 2006). In the political interpretation of the Physiocrats, these principles were translated into a very precise or, as they would often put it, "scientific" economic regime, in which certain mechanisms had to be beyond dispute (Steiner 1998). The Physiocrats therefore did not consider it possible to politically realize the principles of their "new science" under a Montesquieuan system of divided powers. Physiocratic principles for any economy were translatable into concrete maxims and instructions that all members of a society—from emperor to administrator to peasant—should follow rigorously. There could be no balance of powers and interests in their model society, in which the economic rules should be followed strictly and no compromises could be afforded. This further meant that the Physiocrats would not subscribe to the (proto-)sociological approach of appreciating differences in climate, tradition and culture, which was integral to Montesquieu's work.

The importance of observing the same set of laws had consequences for the Physiocratic view on government and again the arguments were linked to the example of China. Referring to the reports by European missionaries based in China, Quesnay argued that "the great empire of China" should serve as "a model for all states" since it was "based upon knowledge of the Natural Law" and thus constituted the realization of "natural order" (Quesnay 2005 [1767], 1010, 1031). By proposing a Chinese model, believed by many contemporaries to generally be based on facts, Quesnay and the Physiocrats thought they had found a way to short-cut complicated debates over constitutional questions. These would normally require prudent arguments about the rise and falls of different states and empires in Europe. As opposed to any European system of government, China's political system, so the Physiocrats and many others argued, had never really fallen. The different "barbarian" tribes that had conquered the empire—Mongols and Manchurians—had always adapted to an ancient and specifically Chinese administrative and economic order. The arguments that the Physiocrats could shape on this background did therefore not necessarily seem utopian to their contemporaries. This was in direct opposition to Montesquieu's constitutional theories, which had labeled China as the perfect example of a "despotic state"—a an assessment based both upon Montesquieu famous climatic theory and upon critical missionary and merchant voices going against the mainstream of positive reports about China (Jacobsen 2012; Demel 1991; Lottes 1991).

Quesnay took the consequence of his disagreement with Montesquieu by developing the concept of legal despotism. Again, the example and ideal for this kind of government was China and thus the attack on Montesquieu was intertwined with praise of this distant empire in his work from 1767, *The Despotism of China*. What is important for the economic context is that the political arguments that Quesnay developed were completely coherent with his economic thesis in *Philosophie Rurale*. This work from 1763 was hitherto the most comprehensive physiocratic treatise of political economy. The points on which Quesnay attacked Montesquieu is not whether or not a sovereign monarch can be moral and just, but how the government can ensure the best possible conditions for the production, that is for agricultural production and the economy in general. Quesnay had such a belief in the nexus between the divine natural order and the best economic laws that it overruled any consideration about different the checks and balances that Montesquieu would propose (see, e.g., Quesnay 2005 [1767], 1009). For Quesnay and his disciples, there existed one principle, one general policy, one economic system that would bring about the greatest advantage for the people.

In the eyes of the Physiocrats this did *not* lead to a democratic development as with the Spinozist radicals of the time as Denis Diderot or Baron d'Holbach (Israel 2010). Rather, it entailed an argument for a single power base (the monarch or emperor) that was obliged to follow the laws. Since the Physiocrats deemed it possible to improve the conditions for a whole population by rigorously adopting this "natural law," the success of any empire rested on the political capability of long-term stability. Thus Quesnay and Mirabeau, another leading Physiocrat, warned against democracy and aristocracy as forms of government simply because these forms of government seemed unable to follow a specific set of maxims continuously (Quesnay 2005 [1767], 1011).

Is it in the different forms of governments imagined by men that we must seek the model for good government? The archetype of the most perfect government, did it not present itself with evidence in the immutable order of the laws of nature, where everything that can be most advantageous to the governing authority and his subjects is upheld by measuring and calculating, and where the positive laws is simply the results of the most complete and most decisive demonstration (Quesnay 2005 [1767], 814).

The strong emphasis on a universal and calculable yardstick for what is "most advantageous" for any government and any population leads us to the third important point for understanding the background to debates on natural order: the conception of science to which this order was linked. In their own understanding, the Physiocrats were on look for the kind of "data" or "facts"—descriptions of both practices and philosophical notions—that would prove an accordance with certain perennial principles. One sympathetic commentator suggested that the physiocratic approach could be labeled *la Science economique demontrée par les faits* (Anonymous Editorial ("K") 1768, 215).[4]

This might sound like a version of an empiricist approach to investigating the economy, but actually the understanding of fact was not as straightforward. Quesnay and other Physiocrats were convinced of the (pre-)existence of a natural order (the result of the natural laws) that could be observed by "the wise" or "the sages" (e.g., Quesnay 2005 [1767], 814, ibid. 2005 [1767], 117). In turn, this belief was based on the kind of "proto-utilitarian" principle the Physiocrats applied to define natural order: Both the moral and physical order is that which is *le plus advantageux aux hommes* (Quesnay 2005 [1767], 115). This firm belief in that all observable data would obey this principle was of course not totally objective. Even in terms of French epistemology in his own time, Quesnay's principles were anomalous. On the one hand, he shared with Étienne Bonnot de Condillac, and other French epistemologists inspired by Locke, the physiological approach of *sensualisme* that wanted to explain human nature with reference to the response to pleasure and pain

---

4 The anonymous author or this, named K, alludes to a work by Le Trosne from 1766.

(Orain 2002; Steiner 1992). On the other hand, Quesnay combined this with the kind of normative explanations for social laws quoted above: the physical and moral order will converge to what is most advantageous the whole species. When Quesnay's proto-utilitarian principles were integrated into a theory of political economy, the Chinese model played a large role as the societal realization of this "normative sensationism" (Steiner 1992, 228). Philippe Steiner discusses the link between this principle and legal despotism in the following manner:

> Legal despotism is the direct result of considerations of natural law: the reference to cooperation between different types of work and to the distribution means that the order of nature and the order of justice are taken into account and that their demands are met. From this point of view, the role played by morality and knowledge in the political constitution of legal despotism is important. Quesnay emphasizes the close connection between morality and politics that, in China, formed but one and the same science (Steiner 1998, 102).

The constitutional counterpart of the physiocratic economic theory thus rested upon an ideal or a utopia, yet one in actual existence in China. Quesnay and the Physiocrats built upon a widely accepted eighteenth-century conviction that China had in fact remained stable under largely unchanged constitution for several millennia (Jacobsen 2012; Demel 1991). Therefore, in their own context, their constitutional ideas for how to improve the economy must be deemed a, somewhat paradoxical, "non-utopian utopia"—ridding the latter concept from the meaning of being a non-place, but retaining its meaning of being an ideal place.

Finally, as for the concept of science in physiocratic theories, the main reference for historians trying to make sense of them should not be the general wave of interest in Newtonian laws of nature that was flourishing in many parts of Europe at Quesnay's time. Rather, one should also or even primarily take into account that in Quesnay's circles there was a general interest in the social interpretation of natural law stemming from the German rationalist tradition (Steiner 1992; Fox-Genovese 1976). Thus, the ambition to combine morality and politics in one science, and claim its practical existence, echoed the writings of G. W. Leibniz and Christian Wolff who both claimed to have found a perfect accordance between their own philosophies and ancient Chinese epistemological and moral principles (Mungello 1977; Ching and

Oxtoby 1992). This line of thought returned in a more political guise as an answer to Montesquieu's political epistemology that rejected any such rationalist and deist premises.[5]

Natural Order in Smith and Quesnay

Adam Smith stayed in Paris from 1764 to 1765, and during that time he came into contact with the Physiocrats. On the Physiocrat's perception of Smith while in Paris, Smith-biographer, Ian S. Ross, writes,

> A leading member of this group [the Physiocrats], Du Pont de Nemours, said they regarded Smith "as a judicious and simple man, but one who had not yet proved his worth." This informant also believed that because of a fear of vested interests there was a discrepancy between Smith's published views in WN and those he asserted in his own quarters, or in those of a friend, "as I have seen him when we were fellow-disciples in the home of M. Quesnay" (Ross 1995, 214).

Smith stayed in contact with several leading Physiocrats through correspondences after his return to Scotland. In Smith's library were thus the works of several prominent Physiocrats, which was published after his year in Paris (Mizuta and Smith 2000). Among these were the collection *Physiocratie* (1767) that Quesnay had personally sent him in 1767 (Ross 1995).

The fact that Smith's visit played a role in the formation of certain basic ideas about political economy is evident in WN. Smith presents Quesnay by describing him as the "very ingenious and profound author" of the physiocratic system, and focuses on the merits of the "arithmetical formularies" in the "Oeconomical Table" (Smith 1976 [1776], ii, 193). Smith explains and praises the physiocratic axiom that the "greatest possible neat [net] product" is preconditioned by distribution of goods "in a state of the most perfect liberty."[6] However, Smith continues, listing different criticisms of the same system (Smith 1976 [1776], ii, 193). The attack is mainly directed against the rigid nature of the political reforms suggested by the Physiocrats, but specifically Smith is skeptical towards the claims that "the class of artificers, man-

---

5 In the physiocratic oevre there is only little traces of direct influence from this rationalist tradition to be found. However, Dupont did praise Wolff as part of a number of "predecessors" to the "science nouvelle" in 1768. Another predecessor was, curiously, also Confucius. See Du Pont de Nemours (1768)

6 On the physiocratic theory of the net product (*produit net*) see e.g. Steiner (2003, 1998)

ufacturers, and merchants, as altogether barren and unproductive" (Smith 1976 [1776], ii, 195). This criticism has often been perceived as Smith's final rejection of the physiocratic doctrines for political economy (e.g. Winch 1996, 114), but after arguing *for* the productivity of the artificers, manufacturers, and merchants, Smith makes an interesting discrepancy as to what he still finds useful in physiocracy.

> This system, however, with all its imperfections is, perhaps, the nearest approximation to the truth that has yet been published upon the subject of political *œconomy*, and is upon that account well worth the considera-tion of every man who wishes to examine with attention the principles of that very important science (Smith 1976 [1776], ii, 199).

Smith's criticism is thus not just directed at the basic assumptions and struc-ture of the physiocratic political economy. Rather, Physiocracy serves as a textbook example in this regard. Smith is torn between on the one hand designating the Physiocrats as a speculative "sect" (Smith 1976 [1776], ii, 200) when it comes to the arguments on the exclusive productivity of farm-ers, while he on the other hand emphasizes the major steps that the Physi-ocrats have made in developing a *science* of political economy. Here, we hit upon an interesting topic that continues to be debated in the Smith litera-ture: how are we to understand Smith's way of balancing the "historical data" with which he compares different world regions with the "truth on political economy" he ascribes to the physiocratic system (see e.g. Aspromourgos 2009, 244ff., Alvey 2003, 239ff.)? The problem arises mainly because the methods for obtaining sources are so different: The readings of historical sources in a Montesquieuan vein keep experimental philosophical principles to a mini-mum, whereas the physiocratic analyses are often based on philosophical and axiomatic reasoning. The text that Smith quotes as "the most distinct and best connected account of this [the physiocratic] doctrine" is Mercier de la Riviére's *L'ordre naturel et essential des societies politiques* from 1767 (Smith 1976 [1776], ii, 200). Smith's close friend, David Hume, was of a completely differ-ent opinion as to the "merits" of the Physiocrats, as testified in a 1769 letter to Abbé Morellet while the latter was writing a book on the political economy of trade:

> I hope that in you work you will thunder them [the Physiocrats], and crush them, and pound then, and reduce them to dust and ashes! They

are, indeed, the set of men the most chimerical and most arrogant that now exist... (Hume [1769] in Smith, Mossner et al. 1977, 114n).

There must have been a further attraction for Smith in *not* going along with the harsh critique of Hume and many others home and abroad (for an account of anti-physiocracy, see Charbit 2000). The fact that Smith praises one specific physiocratic work—*L'Ordre Naturel*—provides an indication of what was the attraction. Mercier de la Riviere had presented Smith with a version of natural order in a rigidly systematic tract, void of the detailed assessment of different laws and institutions of different nations in the world. While Smith was mainly working in the Montesquieuan tradition in terms of political and historical analysis, he obviously saw the need for more speculative lines of thought to complete his own theory on political economy. The Physiocrats, to whom Smith referred on this specific point, had used the model of China to produce a peculiar intermediate between empirical and speculative sources. Thus the natural order—and in fact anything denoted as "natural"—was universal to all states of the world.

Nature, Liberty and Optimism
In his recent work, Istvan Hont has provided crucial insights as to how Smith engaged with the seventeenth century debates on sociability via the works of his teacher Francis Hutcheson, who was opposed to the visions of sociablility (and lack thereof) of both Hobbes and Pufendorf (Hont 2005). Smith outlined three kinds of societies: a society based on fear, a society based on friendship and a society based on commerce. The first was the Hobbesian order that required the controlling power of a Leviathan. The second was a religious vision that Smith would attached to Hutcheson. The third was based on the Pufendorfian approach to sociability and one that would immediately have economic implications (Hont 2005, 39–40). While Pufendorf had on the one hand developed his theory of sociability as a criticism of Hobbes, the commercial solution of Pufendorf's work came from his reading of Dutch jurist Hugo Grotius (Tuck 1999, 142ff.). For the latter, natural law decreed freedom for individuals, corporations and states to communicate, move and exchange and such values were at the center of all Grotius's political concerns. Pufendorf adapted several Grotian arguments into his theories of government and state sovereignty, which subsequently turned on a concept of "natural liberty" (Pufendorf 1991, e.g., 29, 134, 164). Resting on the tradition of natural law, this concept balanced in between a secular and religious under-

standing of how societies could develop benevolently and to the physical benefit of all citizens. And although Smith took quarrels with certain aspects of
Pufendorf's theories about the "state of nature," the concept of natural liberty
became very central in WN (Hont 2005, 159ff.).

The concept of nature has attracted scholarly attention recently as it is
deemed integral to the "secret" and "hidden" theological side of part of
Smith's work (Hill 2004; Alvey 2004; Oslington 2011). This has made the use
of concepts as *nature* and *natural* intimately linked to the debates on the concept of the "invisible hand" (Haldane 2011; Waterman 2002; Brewer 2009).
Using the vocabulary of describing something in society as "natural," these
concepts are familiar to the Western theological tradition which entails a
teleological stance (see Alvey 2003, 6ff.). This is in itself not peculiar. This
is because only the most ardent materialists were developing strictly atheist
political theories at this point in history (see Israel 2010; Waterman 2008).
Therefore, it is the opinion of many latter-day commentators that although
Smith never uses the word "God" in WN and "Deity" only a few times, there is
a theological understanding "lurking" somewhere behind. For Alvey (2003),
this topic is pivotal to the question of optimism versus pessimism in Smith's
work and he argues that both general attitudes are present in Smith's economic theory. On the one hand, there is in Smith's work "an immanent and
historical teleology which can be discerned both in the end given by nature
and in the means of satisfying them" (Alvey 2003, 1). One the other hand,
"Smith indicates that commercial society is neither inevitable nor permanent:
it is not the *telos* of history" (Alvey 2003, 2). In Quesnay's work, the considerations on teleology contained explicit references to a "supreme being" or a
deity in many important passages of his later work. However, the main metaphysical thrust comes into play through the systematic use of natural order.
These metaphysical arguments were a backbone in the optimism concerning
the liberty reforms in French grain trade, even when critics referred to the
(experienced) risk of famine during the implementation of similar reforms
(see Foucault 2007, 344; Kaplan 1976, 687).

The question is, if in Smith's work, the discrepancy between "historical
data," on the one hand, and the notions of a science or a system, on the other,
corresponds to the above-mentioned question of "practical pessimism" vis-à-
vis metaphysical optimism. One indication that there could be such a connection in Smith's work is found in the one passage of WN in which he refers to
metaphysical arguments. Discussing the problem of taxation, he refers to "that
sect of men of letters in France who call themselves The Œconomists" (Smith

1976 [1776], ii, 355) quoting them for the argument that all taxes should "fall ultimately upon the rent of land." This "sect" of "Œconomists" refers to the Physiocrats and Smith takes their argument as an outset for his own investigation of taxation. However, he explicitly seeks to weigh their arguments against a review a large number of past and present practices for taxation rather than "entering into the disagreeable discussion of the metaphysical arguments by which they support their very ingenious theory." As we have seen above, the physiocratic theory of a "single tax" was a point born out of both ideas about economic efficiency *and* the ideological principle that the class of proprietors should *not* have the right to levy taxes (Steiner 2003). As Smith had read *Despotism,* he knew of Quesnay's arguments linking this theory to the model of China. It therefore seems that Smith was implicitly answering to Quesnay's absolute confidence in the integrity of the tax-collecting mandarins in China when stating later in the section on taxation practices that "[t]he mandarins and other tax-gatherers will, no doubt, find their advantage in continuing the practice of a payment which is so much more liable to abuse than any payment in money" (Smith 1976 [1776], ii, 364–65).

Smith's reaction to the physiocratic praise of China can be interpreted in the light of what contemporary Scotch thinker Adam Ferguson had written on China in the 1760s. Ferguson acknowledged the stability and complexity of Chinese governance, but thought of it as the epitome of an imperial system that was void of any proper civil society. The bureaucratic system meant that any person engaged in governance was but a professionalized and compartmentalized administrator who was secluded thoroughly from the real political concerns (Hill 2006, 170). To Fergusons mind, the only "great object of the government" consisted in "raising and consuming the fruits of the earth" (Ferguson 1768 [1767], 347–48). Although this sounded similar to the physiocratic agenda, with its strong focus on agriculture, Ferguson had a very different societal order in mind. Principles of active citizenship, which necessitated smaller communities, were at the core of Ferguson's political theories, and this weighed much greater than any promises for great economic advances for large number of peoples.

As opposed to Ferguson, Smith agreed with the Physiocrats that the "prosperity of any country" should be measured by the "increase of the number of inhabitants" (Smith 1976 [1776], i, 79). Smith did share with Ferguson a focus on the civic virtues tied to the direct participation in political development, Smith had economic indicators for progress or stability. But although he recognized, for example, the positive economic function of the mandarin tax gathering in theory, Smith did not share the Physiocrat's trust in the convergence of theory and practice in this aspect of the Chinese economy. On the other hand, the quote above testifies to the fact that Smith was aware of the "metaphysical arguments" that served as a foundation for the political economy of the Physiocrats. It seems that the question for Smith was to choose carefully which metaphysical arguments to employ. When the metaphysical arguments seemed to warrant exaggerated optimism for the effect of concrete state practices, Smith wanted to rely on empirical evidence, but in order to deliver a normative and systematic message on the future of political economy, he seemed willing to engage with certain metaphysical categories. This was the double character of the physiocratic notion of natural order represented to Smith. While being the basic economic principle in Lemercier's system, the ingenuity of which Smith praised, natural order also represented the danger of too great a political control of society.

Precise Regimen vs. Natural Liberty
In a short chapter of WN, "Of the Natural Progress of Opulence," Smith presents a concise vision of how all societies must go through the same stages of economic development. This is an example of Smith's more overarching theoretical considerations, in which there is less empirical data and more theoretical considerations to be found. He expands the basic assumption of the Physiocrats that agriculture must serve as the basis of every society:

> According to the natural course of things, therefore, the greater part of the capital of every growing society is, first, directed to agriculture, afterwards to manufactures, and last of all to foreign commerce. This order of things is so very natural that in every society that had any territory it has always, I believe, been in some degree observed (Smith 1976 [1776], I, 405).

From this, seems clear that Smith applies the notion of "the natural course of things" as a fundamental principle that drives the economy of "every growing society"—i.e. a society on the benevolent path to increasing its wealth. As such, it is different from how he had used this specific phrase in the TMS, in which it would rather denote the forces of nature as a disturbance or contrary force to what the "sentiments of mankind" (Smith 1767, 241). In WN, this "natural course" is integral to Smith's theory and universally applicable to societies all over the world. Thus, in the paragraphs before the above quote from WN, Smith's uses "natural course of things" as synonymous with "natural order of things":

> But though this natural order of things must have taken place in some degree in every such society, it has, in all the modern states of Europe, been, in many respects, entirely inverted. The foreign commerce of some of their cities has introduced all their finer manufactures, or such as were fit for distant sale; and manufactures and foreign commerce together have given birth to the principal improvements of agriculture. The manners and customs which the nature of their original government introduced, and which remained after that government was greatly altered, necessarily forced them into this unnatural and retrograde order (Smith 1976 [1776], i, 405–6).

This is an example of Smith giving normative assessments on a historical scale. The argument infers a universalized concept of the "natural order", which is the very opposite of the "unnatural and retrograde order," in which the fundamental laws of economic development have been disturbed. The structure of these arguments seem almost identical with the physiocratic doctrines, but Smith explicitly points out that one cannot simply assume his understanding of "natural order" to be congruent with that of the Physiocrats, but rather than entering into the debate of which specific model should be used for governing, he questions the physiocratic interpretation of what an economic model can be used for politically. He criticizes Quesnay's understanding of the economy of the "political body," stating that,

> [Quesnay] imagined that it would thrive and prosper only under a certain precise regimen, the exact regimen of perfect liberty and perfect justice. He seems not to have considered that, in the political body, the natural effort which every man is continually making to better his own condition is a principle of preservation capable of preventing and correcting, in many respects, the bad effects of a political *œconomy*, in some degree, both partial and oppressive. Such a political *œconomy*, though it no doubt retards more or less, is not always capable of stopping altogether the natural progress of a nation towards wealth and prosperity, and still less of making it go backwards. If a nation could not prosper without the enjoyment of perfect liberty and perfect justice, there is not in the world

a nation which could ever have prospered. In the political body, however, the wisdom of nature has fortunately made ample provision for remedying many of the bad effects of the folly and injustice of man ... (Smith 1976 [1776], ii, 194–95).

For Smith, there is no such thing as a precise regimen that can give the perfect solution to any situation that the political economy of a state will face. The "natural efforts of every man" seems to correlate with the "propensity" of "human nature" to "truck, barter and exchange" with which Smith has famously explained the origins of the division of labor (Smith 1976 [1776], i, 17). Here, Smith had made it clear that it is such a propensity and *not* "the effect of any human wisdom" that makes the division of labor arise and secure "general opulence." At this point, Smith only explains the negation—it is *not* the human intention and wisdom that gave us the division of labor—and by leaving it at that, it seems like a rather simple reference to a deity or a creator, which is needed to complete the theory. However, Smith seems to have been rather selective in deciding when to make this kind of reference and it has a very precise argumentative function. Just as there is a dichotomy between "human wisdom" and "the wisdom of nature," there is a clear difference between "perfect liberty"—ascribed to the Physiocrats—and "natural liberty." "Natural liberty" is a concept that Smith sets into play in his when explaining defining his legislative ideal.

All systems either of preference or of restraint, therefore, being thus completely taken away, the obvious and simple system of natural liberty establishes itself of its own accord. Every man, as long as he does not violate the laws of justice, is left perfectly free to pursue his own interest his own way, and to bring both his industry and capital into competition with those of any other man, or order of men. The sovereign is completely discharged from a duty, in the attempting to perform which he must always be exposed to innumerable delusions, and for the proper performance of which no human wisdom or knowledge could ever be sufficient; the duty of superintending the industry of private people, and of directing it towards the employments most suitable to the interest of the society (Smith 1976 [1776], ii, 208).

To understand what Smith was revolting against, it is necessary to look more closely at the physiocratic conception of the role of the legislator. The Physiocrats had allowed themselves to theorize about the natural order as a legislative ideal—in a set of concrete rules—for political economy. Thus, political economy could be perfected if certain rules and maxims were followed. When criticized publically for this belief *and* its connection to the Chinese model by Gabriel Bonnot de Mably (see Jacobsen 2012), the response on this point in the editorial of *Ephémérides*—the main journal of the Physiocrats— was as follows:

> We regard, Monsieur [Mably], the Chinese government as the best government which exists, but not as the best government possible (in Pinot 1906, 211).

To this extent, while China had provided a model for political economy in Quesnay's work, the model could still be further perfected. It is the *way* in which this perfection or betterment could be achieved that Smith takes issues with. While Smith subscribes to many physiocratic lines of argument, especially those regarding free competition in trade, he is constantly on guard when it comes to theories about legislation and implementation. What Quesnay had found in the Chinese model were specific maxims for governing, which he thought to be in line with an age-old philosophical tradition. These principles varied in specificity from the correct abstract understanding of how heaven and earth were connected and down to how children should treat their parents and how much people should be taxed. The specific *rules* that must be abided are important and only if they are acknowledged by an elite would the state become opulent. As we have seen, Quesnay was convinced that generally both the emperors and the mandarins in China had the sufficient skills and wisdom to rule according to natural law.

What complicates matters further, however, is that the rules Quesnay wants to promote are not expected to steer the course to opulence through ongoing regulation, but to secure the maximum freedom of trade and competition on the markets.[7] Explaining the French legacy of the physiocratic version of *philosophie* économique, Faccarello and Steiner have pointed to the argument of Quesnay and other French liberalists that "spontaneous harmonisation does not exist in those fields where the social mechanism of competition cannot work" (Faccarello and Steiner 2008, 18). However, what *does* always

---

7 A point on which Quesnay has had a strong impact on subsequent generations of liberal French political economist (see Faccarello and Steiner 2008).

exist for the Physiocrats, as I showed above, is the *order*, but perceived as an abstract understanding that can be acknowledged by certain "sages"—a word that Quesnay used to describe those who had acknowledged the universal economic principles of any society (Jacobsen 2012). What Quesnay found in China was a model for the legislative relation to the natural order. According to him, the Chinese political and philosophical tradition attested an admirable attention to conforming "positive", or actual, laws to the natural laws that bring about natural order (see Quesnay 2005 [1767], 1083–84). Therefore, legislation should not necessarily be lax if natural order had not yet been attained. While the Physiocrats recognized that market competition and societal harmonization could seem like opposite forces, Faccarello and Steiner explain that in the *philosophie* économique,

> ... the role of the legislator is to create a political structure that enables these interests to be recognised as identical. When they are not identical, the legislator has to construct a system of laws; for the legislator can become manipulative and dangerous if not guided by the knowledge of general rules discovered by *philosophie économique*... (Faccarello and Steiner 2008, 18).

The model of China gave the Physiocrats a reason to believe in the universality of their own philosophic-economical discoveries that specific maxims or policies could and should generally be applied anywhere. For Smith, the Chinese model of the Physiocrats (or "the evidential perfectible model," as Smith seems to have thought of it). In Mirabeau's speech at Quesnay's funeral, the discovery of the *produit net* was explained as the latter's theoretical contribution to a universal tradition of understanding economics reaching back to Chinese antiquity (Maverick 1946). For Smith, the Chinese model of the Physiocrats was be the very antithesis to his political-economic theory of non-interference; it was based on a state that had been governed successfully according to a set a specific set of maxims for millennia. This was a state in which the duty of the sovereign was to "superintend" and control many aspects of trade and—what Smith universally warns against in political economy—direct the industry "towards the employments most suitable to the interest of the society" (Smith 1976 [1776], ii, 208).

For Quesnay and the Physiocrats, the role of economic ideas was active in society to a whole different degree than in Smith. When describing their political model, through the ideal of China, there were numerous reflections on how to specifically instruct the people—even in rural areas—of certain rules or maxims that they should abide by. On a higher level of social order, Quesnay's own "maxims" were supposed to function similarly, instructing administrative agents on how to govern. While, on the one hand, Quesnay and Mirabeau would write in *Philosophie Rurale* about the "magic of a well ordered society" (in Skinner 1996, 128) then, on the other hand, this order could not be expected to occur about ex nihilo or as a "natural course of things" as Smith would put it.

The interesting thing is that Smith and Quesnay did not differ very much in what they saw as the basic correct measures for generating state opulence. The laissez-faire-principle of the Physiocrats demanded, just as in Smith's work, free and unlimited trade and competition on everything produced in a state. In order to argue properly for his views on non-interfering governance in the light of the physiocratic optimism for a "precise regimen," Smith presents an "abstracted optimism" with regard to "nature's wisdom;" everything that is described as *natural* finds a counterpart in the actual tendencies in his contemporary European states. Here, one can identify in WN an opposite "practical pessimism" in terms of economic consequences of the legislative development of these states. This may be interepreted as an example where the invisible hand has been put to the side and a (most likely arbitrary) will of sovereign is in control instead. The result is "unnatural" and opposed to the invisible hand's "naturalness." Precisely because it is legitimate for Smith to retain the abstract optimism, he can theorize about what "the natural" may consist of (for a detailed account see Waterman 2002).

The Physiocrats had allowed themselves to theorize about the natural order as a legislative ideal—in a set of concrete rules—for political economy. Indeed, they had seen this political theory as a necessary part of their system. Smith, on the other hand, raised the "laissez-faire"-approach from a practical question of forcing through free trade to an argument for less political interference, which found support mainly on the abstract level of the invisible hand and other notions of the non-human. In this way, he did not share the Physiocrat's risk of political critique, while still being able to use to overall framework for assuming universal principles for any economic system.

Conclusion: "Scottish Perfectibility" before and after Smith
Knud Haakonssen has argued that Smith stood out from the mainstream of Scottish thinkers for whom questions of human education and perfectibility were at the center of moral thought (Haakonssen 2003, 213–14). However,

where Haakonssen argues that these topics were absent in Smith's argumentation all together, the above discussion of Smith's relation to the conception of the physiocratic "perfect regimen," gives us reason to think about the dynamics of Smith's discussion of the Physiocrats. His explicit rejection of certain political components does not mean that they did not have an impact on the way Smith formulated his ideas on ordering society. In fact, the above would lead us to think that Smith needed a proper alternative to the theoretical basis of the physiocratic understanding of natural order. Smith's work needs to be interpreted not only in relation to the Scottish debates on justice and jurisprudence, but also in the light of the problems for political economy that Smith was negotiating in relation to impulses from France. In fact, Smith's treatment of these of "perfect liberty" and "precise regimen"—although he was critical of the physiocratic answer—seems to have provided him with important concepts for the normative side of his political economy. Thus, by juxtaposing perfected "human wisdom" with "the wisdom of nature," Smith found a way in which his empirical analysis could transcend the level of historical data, of which he presents so much in WN. Although this is not the same kind of argumentation as what was at play in Quesnay's use of the Chinese model for specific maxims, Smith does search for a level of argumentation that can convince his readers of the blessings of freedom of trade. Smith's specific reference to physiocratic paradigms—"natural order" most prominently—as a stepping stone for reaching this optimist trust in the workings of "nature's wisdom" connects the two theories on this level. And since, as I have hopefully shown, the Physiocrats used the model of China to reach *their* optimist position, the employment of this extra-European reference seems to have consequences beyond their own theory. The very fact that Quesnay argued that he had found a perfectible model (but non-Utopian, i.e., *real*) was a useful piece in the puzzle of formulating a science of political economy. When Smith argues specifically that "nature's wisdom" is in fact even more flexible and effective than Quesnay believed in the light of his perfect model, Smith's optimism is an abstract radicalization of physiocratic non-utopian modelized optimism.

As testified by the case of Francis Horner, Smith's attempt to use the physiocratic system in this manner did not go unnoticed by his own students. In fact, his first biographer Dugald Stewart, himself an influential political economist and Horner's teacher, sought to defend the merit of the physiocratic universalistic theory in the face of Smith's critique. Stewart reached a compromise, stating that

... if, on the One hand, the language of the Economist be more precise and definite, and the result of more accurate metaphysical analysis than that of Mr Smith, and if some of the fundamental principles of the former are of more specific nature, and more universal application, the doctrines inculcated in the Wealth of Nations are, on the other hand, with very few exceptions, of greater practical utility to those who are engaged in the general business of the world, especially those who have a more particular reference to the business of political life (in Winch, Collini, and Burrow 1983, 50).

Quoting other passages from Stewart's work, Winch, Collini and Burrow showcase the general understanding of the French *Économistes* in Stewart's generation of Scottish economists. A closer look at Stewart's analysis makes it clear that a point on which the physiocratic theory continued to be attractive was specifically the question how to represent an economic model for social order:

[T]hey [the *Économistes*] had accomplished the first task of any science of politics by describing what would constitute the "ideal perfection of the social order" and how it could be realized by legislation. This ideal represented a limit, in the mathematical sense, "towards which governments may be expected to approach nearer and nearer as the triumphs of philosophy extend." But this limit or ideal should not be confused with earlier "Utopian plans of government" which depicted political order as a problem for "human contrivance" and "skilful management," usually requiring "a miraculous reformation in the moral character of a people." It recognized that good morals were the *effect* of good laws rather than a precondition for them (Winch, Collini and Burrow 1983, 35).

Stewart addressed the topic of "perfection" and related it closely to a point or limit to which governments, without deploying a utopian imagination, should converge. The clear-cut rejection of the legacy of the Physiocrats being utopian is very relevant, since it indicates that their own combination of arguments of mathematical, philosophical and cultural origin had an effect beyond Smith. Smith's fragile construction of finding a middle ground between historical data—"the business of the world" in Stewarts terms—and "metaphysical analysis" was not entirely convincing to Stewart who found the potential for "universal application" greater in the tradition after the Physiocrats than in Smith's work. Together, however, these different strands of theories pushed very forcefully the shared agenda for removing hindrances to free trade. Although the Chinese model had no role in that particular debate, it had served as the lens through which the Physiocrats had originally developed a universal notion of natural order, of which the functionality could thus be empirically proved. Smith, Stewart and other economist of the period were able to use these arguments as a stepping stone for pushing a debate on economic orders that would not need the "precise regimen" of a state to uphold itself as opposed to Quesnay who had thought this was a necessary relation in the case of China. Here, natural order was liberated from the context of the state and was at work in any commercial relation between "men, or orders of men" as Smith put it. The expansion of the political imagination with a supposed "non-Utopian Utopia" or a perfectible model—the Chinese model specifically—had been an important step in this process.

While for the Physiocrats, this perfectible model was a precondition for reaching a proper level of scientifically based governance, Smith saw the belief in this perfection as an impediment to the development of national wealth. Rather, he would rely on certain organizing qualities present at all times and *spontaneously* in any state of sociability—though one could add the concept of spontaneity in hindsight and as an analytical category only. The Physiocrats had sought to ground their metaphysical beliefs in a rationalist formula that lead to specific maxims. They needed to explain just how the "magic" of the system would be brought about—that is, how people's self-interest would work for the commonwealth. As opposed to his Scottish successors, Smith rejected the basic tenets of the physiocratic explanation on this specific point. His motivations were grounded both in constitutional opinions—doubting the administrative benevolence of any state power—and a fondness of leaving space for a deistic undercurrent in the (civil) society. However powerful an economic notion this "space of spontaneity" became, once it was coupled with biologist notions of selection and development, the dynamism and openness that has since been ascribed to Smith's explanation of economic orders cannot be disjointed from an older, theologically inspired tradition of natural liberty.

References

Alvey, J. E. 2003. *Adam Smith: Optimist or Pessimist? A New Problem Concerning the Teleological Basis of the Commercial Society.* Aldershot: Ashgate Publishing Group.

————. 2004. "The Secret, Natural, Theological Foundation of Adam Smith's Work." *Journal of Markets and Morality* 7, no. 2: 335–61.

Brewer, A. 2009. "On the Other (Invisible) Hand." *History of Political Economy* 41, no. 3: 519–43.

Ching, J., and W. G. Oxtoby. 1992. "Introduction." In *Moral Enlightenment: Leibniz and Wolff on China,* edited by Julia Ching and Willard Gurdon Oxtoby. Sankt Augustin; Nettetal: Institut Monumenta Serica; Steyler.

Coleman, W. O. 2002. *Economics and Its Enemies: Two Centuries of Anti-Economics.* Houndmills, Basingstoke, Hampshire, New York: Palgrave Macmillan.

Demel, W. 1991. "China in the Political Thought of Western and Central Europe 1570–1750." In *China and Europe: Images and Influences in Sixteenth to Eighteenth Centuries,* edited by Thomas H. C. Lee. Hong Kong: Chinese University Press.

Du Pont de Nemours, P. S. 1768. *De L'origine Et Des Progrès D'une Science Nouvelle.* Londres; Et se trouve a Paris: Chez Desaint.

Faccarello, G., and P. Steiner. 2008. "Interest, Sensationism and the Science of the Legislator: French 'Philosophie Économique', 1695–1830." *The European Journal of the History of Economic Thought* 15, no. 1:1.

Ferguson, A. 1768 [1767]. *An Essay on the History of Civil Society by Adam Ferguson.* London: Printed for A. Millar and T. Cadell; and A. Kincaid and J. Bell, Edinburgh.

Foucault, M. 2007. *Security, Territory, Population: Lectures at the Collège De France, 1977–78.* Basingstoke; New York: Palgrave Macmillan: République Française.

Fox-Genovese, E. 1976. *The Origins of Physiocracy: Economic Revolution and Social Order in Eighteenth-Century France.* Ithaca, NY: Cornell University Press.

Fry, M. 1992. *Adam Smith's Legacy: His Place in the Development of Modern Economics.* London and New York: Routledge.

Gwartney, J. D. 2009. *Macroeconomics: Private and Public Choice.* Mason, OH: South-Western Cengage Learning.

Haakonssen, K. 2003. "Natural Jurisprudence and the Theory of Justice." In *The Cambridge Companion to the Scottish Enlightenment,* edited by A. Broadie. Cambridge: Cambridge University Press.

Haldane, J. 2011. "Smith, Theology and Natural Law Ethics." In *Adam Smith as Theologian*, edited by Paul Oslington. New York: Routledge.

Hamowy, R. 1987. *The Scottish Enlightenment and the Theory of Spontaneous Order.* Carbondale: Southern Illinois University Press.

Hayek, F. A. 1978. *New Studies in Philosophy, Politics, Economics and the History of Ideas.* Chicago: University of Chicago Press.

Hill, L. 2004. "Further Reflections on the 'Hidden Theology' of Adam Smith." *The European Journal of the History of Economic Thought* 11, no. 4: 629–35.

———. 2006. *The Passionate Society the Social, Political and Moral Thought of Adam Ferguson.* Dordrecht, the Netherlands: Springer.

Hirschman, A. O. 1977. *The Passions and the Interests: Political Arguments for Capitalism before Its Triumph.* Princeton, NJ: Princeton University Press.

Hont, I. 2005. *Jealousy of Trade: International Competition and the Nation State in Historical Perspective.* Cambridge, MA: Belknap Press of Harvard University Press.

Horner, F. 1814. "Review of M. Canard, Principes D'économie Politique " *The Edinburgh Review* 48, no. 95.

Hunter, I. 2001. *Rival Enlightenments: Civil and Metaphysical Philosophy in Early Modern Germany.* Cambridge, UK and New York: Cambridge University Press.

———. 2003. "The Love of a Sage, or, the Command of a Superior: The Natural Law Doctrines of Leibniz and Pufendorf." In *Early Modern Natural Law Theories: Contexts and Strategies in the Early Enlightenment*, edited by T. J. Hochstrasser and Peter Schröder, 169–94. Dordrecht: Kluwer Academic Publishers.

Israel, J. 2010. *A Revolution of the Mind: Radical Enlightenment and the Intellectual Origins of Modern Democracy.* Princeton, NJ: Princeton University Press.

Jacobsen, S. G. 2012. "Physiocracy and the Chinese Model: Enlightened Lessons from China's Political Economy?" In *Thoughts on Economic Development in China*, edited by Ying Ma and Hans-Michael Trautwein. London: Routledge.

K, [Anonymous]. 1768. "Voyages d'un Philosophe [review]." *In Ephémérides du citoyen, ou Bibliothèque raisonnée des sciences morales et politiques*, edited by Nicolas Baudeau. Paris: Lacombe.

Kaplan, S. L. 1976. *Bread, Politics and Political Economy in the Reign of Louis Xv, International Archives of the History of Ideas* 86. The Hague: Martinus Nijhoff.

Larrère, C. 1992. *L'invention De L'économie Au Xviiie Siècle: Du Droit Naturel À La Physiocratie, Léviathan.* Paris: Presses universitaires de France.

Lottes, G. 1991. "China European Political Thought 1750–1850." In *China and Europe: Images and Influences in Sixteenth to Eighteenth Centuries,* edited by Thomas H. C. Lee, 65. Hong Kong: Chinese University Press.

Maverick, L. A. 1946. "Introduction." In *China a Model for Europe: Lewis A. Maverick. A Translation of François Quesnay's "Le Despotisme De La Chine", Paris, 1767,* edited by Lewis Adams Maverick. San Antonio, TX: P. Anderson.

Meek, R. L. 1963. *The Economics of Physiocracy; Essays and Translations.* vol. 2, *University of Glasgow Social and Economic Studies,* n.s. Cambridge, MA: Harvard University Press.

Mizuta, H., and A. Smith. 2000. *Adam Smith's Library: A Catalogue.* Rev ed. Oxford and New York: Clarendon Press; Oxford University Press.

Mungello, D. E. 1977. *Leibniz and Confucianism, the Search for Accord.* Honolulu: University Press of Hawaii.

Orain, A. 2002. "Condillac Face a La Physiocratie: Terre, Valeur Et Repartition." *Revue economique* 53: 1075–99.

Oslington, P. 2011. "Introduction: Theological Readings of Adam Smith." In *Adam Smith as Theologian,* edited by Paul Oslington. New York: Routledge.

Oz-Salzberger, F. 2003. "The Political Theory of the Scottish Enlightenment." In *The Cambridge Companion to the Scottish Enlightenment,* edited by A. Broadie. Cambridge: Cambridge University Press.

Petsoulas, C. 2001. *Hayek's Liberalism and Its Origins: His Idea of Spontaneous Order and the Scottish Enlighenment.* London and New York: Routledge.

Pinot, V. 1906. "Les Physiocrates Et La Chine Au Xviiie Siecle." *Revue d'histoire moderne et contemporaine* 8.

Porter, R. 2003. *The Cambridge History of Science. Volume 4, Eighteenth-Century Science.* Cambridge: Cambridge University Press.

Pufendorf, S. 1991. *Pufendorf: On the Duty of Man and Citizen According to Natural Law.* Cambridge: Cambridge University Press.

Quesnay, F. 2005 [1767]. "Le Despotisme De La Chine." In *Oeuvres économiques complètes et autres textes,* edited by Christine Théré, Loïc Charles and Jean-Claude Perrot. Paris: INED. Institut national d'études démographiques.

Reill, P. H. 2005. *Vitalizing Nature in the Enlightenment.* Berkeley: University of California Press.

Skinner, A. S. 1996. *A System of Social Science: Papers Relating to Adam Smith.* Oxford and New York: Clarendon Press; Oxford University Press.

Smith, A. 1767. *The Theory of Moral Sentiments to Which Is Added a Dissertation on the Origin of Languages*. London: Printed for A. Millar, A. Kincaid and J. Bell, and sold by T. Cadell.

————. 1976 [1776]. *An Inquiry into the Nature and Causes of the Wealth of Nations*. Chicago: University of Chicago Press.

Smith, C. 2006. *Adam Smith's Political Philosophy: The Invisible Hand and Spontaneous Order*. Routledge Studies in Social and Political Thought. London and New York: Routledge.

Steiner, P. 1992. "L'économie politique du Royaume Agricole: François Quesnay." In *Nouvelle histoire de la pensée économique*, edited by Gilbert Faccarello and Alain Béraud. Paris: La Découverte.

————. 1998. *La «Science Nouvelle» De L'économie Politique* 96, *Philosophies*. Paris: Presses universitaires de France.

————. 2003. "Physiocracy and French Pre-Classical Political Economy." In *A Companion to the History of Economic Thought*, edited by Warren J. Samuels, Jeff Biddle, and John Bryan Davis. Malden, MA: Blackwell.

Stollberg-Rilinger, B. 1986. *Der Staat als Maschine : Zur politischen Metaphorik des Absoluten Fürstenstaats*. Berlin: Duncker & Humblot.

Tuck, R. 1999. *The Rights of War and Peace: Political Thought and the International Order from Grotius to Kant*. Oxford and New York: Oxford University Press.

Vaggi, G. 1987. *The Economics of François Quesnay*. Basingstoke: Macmillan Press.

Waterman, A. M. C. 2002. "Economics as Theology: Adam Smith's Wealth of Nations." *Southern Economic Journal* 68, no. 4:907–21.

————. 2008. "The Changing Theological Context of Economic Analysis since the Eighteenth Century." *History of Political Economy* no. 40.

Winch, D. 1996. *Riches and Poverty: An Intellectual History of Political Economy in Britain, 1750–1834*. Cambridge, UK, and New York: Cambridge University Press.

Winch, D., S. Collini, and J. W. Burrow. 1983. *That Noble Science of Politics: A Study in Nineteenth-Century Intellectual History*. Cambridge, UK, and New York: Cambridge University Press.

Wootton, D. 2006. "Liberty, Metaphor, and Mechanism: 'Checks and Balances' and the Origins of Modern Constitutionalism." In *Liberty and American Experience in the Eighteenth Century*, edited by David Womersley. Indianapolis: Liberty Fund.

Young, J. T. 2008. "Law and Economics in the Protestant Natural Law Tradition: Samuel Pufendorf, Francis Hutcheson, and Adam Smith." *Journal of the History of Economic Thought* 30, no. 3: 283–96.

Qualitative Capitalism and Continental Critique
Émigré Social Scientists Encounter the American Consumer, 1933–45

Joseph Malherek[1]

I

"You know as an old Viennese socialist I really felt completely at home with the New Deal—with the Roosevelt administration," recalled the émigré social scientist and market researcher Paul F. Lazarsfeld in reference to one of his early assignments in the United States (Morrison 1988, 192). Lazarsfeld's socialist politics demanded a keen interest in problems of labor and unemployment, but his leftist disposition also compelled an extraordinary comprehension of social stratification. This had a direct application in the commercial, capitalistic world of market research. The experience of a cohort of European émigré social researchers, led by Lazarsfeld, who became involved in market research, media analysis, and mass culture criticism in the interwar period in the U.S. demonstrates the creative application of socialist and psychoanalytic insights to capitalism's problems with its mysterious markets, often composed of unknown groups of individuals with inscrutable motivations. The study of consumer markets—as an applied form of social research, more broadly—provided a venue for socialists and liberal capitalists alike to practice their methods in a manageable forum. The Viennese social psychologists Lazarsfeld and Ernest Dichter, colleagues of different political persuasions, both channeled an interest in human motivations and decision-making into institutional programs of market research that had immediate applicability in the American context. The so-called "Frankfurt School" of critical theorists, including Theodor W. Adorno and Leo Lowenthal, meanwhile developed a radical critique of mass media and mass culture while involved a project organized around the applied science of market research. Lazarsfeld, a committed socialist from his youth, consciously applied socialism's urgent concern with social stratification to contempo-

---

1 Joseph Malherek is a Ph.D. candidate in American Studies at George Washington University.

rary marketing problems, and he built institutions that employed Dichter, Adorno, and Lowenthal as they developed their own alternative methodologies. While Lazarsfeld, a mathematician by training, used market research as venue to develop his quantitative methods, many in his institutes practiced qualitative inquiry, and many of the Frankfurt scholars fiercely clashed with Lazarsfeld, resisting the positivistic tendencies of empirical social science. However, Lazarsfeld was the central figure in this cohort of émigrés, providing the institutional home for the development of Continental critiques of capitalism that were, paradoxically, integrated with the practical science of market research. This "intellectual migration," as Donald Fleming and Bernard Bailyn (1969) aptly describe it, thus also had a material component: the economic ideas of these émigrés, both critical and analytical, produced important knowledge market of segments and consumer subjects that had commercial applications.

David Morrison (1998, 40), a Lazarsfeld expert, writes that "one would look in vain in Lazarsfeld's work for the type of political intervention through scholarship that is the associated mark of academics who are Marxist." Morrison submits that Lazarsfeld's work may seem to "float" on a "residue of socialist sentiment," but that background is nevertheless incongruous with his close ties to corporate America. Lazarsfeld's defense that his "trivial" market studies were useful in the development of concepts is dismissed by Morrison as a rationalization or "convenient gloss" (Morrison 1998, 97). There is no doubt that an activist socialist or progressive politics largely disappeared from Lazarsfeld's work in the U.S., and this conspicuous absence alienated his more committed friends and colleagues like the sociologist Robert Lynd, who had done much to advance Lazarsfeld's career (Smith 1994). But what remained of Lazarsfeld's socialism was evident not in an overt politics, but rather in his sophisticated analysis of social stratification which, when translated into market research, meant an understanding of market segments and the motivations of consumers from different social strata. Other scholars engaged in different disciplinary debates, such as Peter Simonson and Gabriel Weimann (2003, 14), have sought to reassess Lazarsfeld's reputation in media studies as the father of the "dominant paradigm" of "limited media effects." They do so by drawing out some elements of critical theory, or at least expressions of sympathy toward that mode of inquiry, in Lazarsfeld's work and in his professional relationships. But the most salient element of Lazarsfeld's Continental, socialist background was not an overt expression but rather a formal mode of interpretation that produced an extraordinary comprehension of social stratification. This was a key socialist concern that Lazarsfeld applied—absent its implications for class conflict—in the commercial world as an analysis of market segments. By examining the trajectory of Lazarsfeld's early career, in contrast to his colleagues Adorno, a severe critic of capitalism, and Dichter, a celebrant of commercial hedonism, one can appreciate how the European ideas of socialism and psychoanalysis had commercial applications in burgeoning consumer culture of the U.S.

II

Lazarsfeld's socialist background was fundamental to the development of his method of social research; in many ways it provided the trajectory for his career, including the commercial applications of his work. Hans Zeisel—Lazarsfeld's longtime friend, colleague in social research, and a fellow émigré—in recalling their years together in Vienna, emphasized that while he and Lazarsfeld had diverse personal influences, including Alfred Adler and their psychology teachers at the University of Vienna, Karl and Charlotte Bühler, the most immediately influential force in their lives was the Austrian socialist party, a movement that was "messianic and enormously practical" (Zeisel 1979, 10). "At the core of Paul's endeavors," wrote Zeisel, alluding to the commitments of a historical materialist, "was the enormous desire to understand human motivation...and how social structures, both present and past, grow, change, and disappear" (Zeisel 1979, 14). Another friend and colleague, the American sociologist David Riesman, who cited the Lazarsfeld cohort's work as a major influence on his famous midcentury sociological studies, *The Lonely Crowd* and *Faces in the Crowd*, agreed: "[H]e had a lifelong nostalgia for socialism, Vienna style, disguised in what seemed the ultra-American regalia of an empirically minded institution-building, intellectually adventurous, and wide ranging social scientist" (Riesman 1979, 226–27). Lazarsfeld himself, in his memoir, recalled his activity in the Socialist Student Movement in Vienna after the First World War, and its influence on his work: "We were concerned with why our propaganda was unsuccessful, and wanted to conduct psychological studies to explain it" (Lazarsfeld 1969, 272). Lazarsfeld was not only a committed socialist, but also a determined institution-builder who sought to organize his comrades as activist social researchers.[2]

That Lazarsfeld was able to channel his desire for social progress into insti-

---

2 "I was very active in the socialist youth movement," recalled Lazarsfeld. "It was really ... almost transferring my clique of younger people ... into this whole [research] activity" (quoted in Morrison [1998, 19]).

tutional forms with broad applications beyond the realm of socialist politics is partly the result of his ambition and fascination with the methods of social research, and partly because of the European crisis that produced an exile community forced to adapt to radically new circumstances. Lazarsfeld was born in Vienna in 1901 to secular-Jewish, socialist-intellectual parents: his father was a lawyer and his mother was a psychologist, and both were published authors. Lazarsfeld came of age during the First World War and, in its wake, the birth of the new republic in Austria under the rule of the Social Democrats, the "natural home" of the Jew, according to Morrison, for its ideology of brotherhood and internationalism that acted as a "buffer" against anti-Semitism (Morrison 1998, 25–26). Lazarsfeld was active politically as a young man, writing regularly for the monthly journal of the Social Democratic Party, *Der Kampf Sozialdemokratische Monatschrift*, to which the likes of Leon Trotsky and Karl Kautsky contributed (Morrison 1998, 38). He also formed a league of socialist students and later organized socialist summer and winter camps for youth. In 1923, while he was still a student at the University of Vienna, on the path to earning a doctorate in applied mathematics, the Bühlers were appointed to establish a department of psychology, and young Paul would sit in on their seminars. Paul Neurath, founder of the Lazarsfeld archive at the University of Vienna, observed that the political climate of the time was such that socialist intellectuals like Lazarsfeld were drawn to psychology and psychoanalysis because they wanted "to participate in the creation of the new man for the new socialist society." Lazarsfeld impressed his mentor Charlotte Bühler when he shared with her his sophisticated statistical analysis of some questionnaires filled out by proletarian youth, which he acquired from a leader of the Socialist Young Workers who appealed to the rhetoric of workers but failed to see the meaning in quantifiable data.[3] This novel presentation convinced Bühler to appoint Lazarsfeld as her assistant, and later as a teacher of statistics and social psychology (Neurath 1981, 6). Lazarsfeld was inspired by the physicist Friedrich Adler, son of the founder of the Social Democratic Party, antiwar political assassin, and close friend of the Lazarsfeld family (Morrison 1998, 36). Adler encouraged the young Lazarsfeld's interest in mathematics, which had great prestige among Austro-Marxists who were attempting to merge social science and mathematics in the service of social progress (Zeisel 1979, 10). Lazarsfeld's political commitment

---

3 "[H]e was just interested in their misery, you see," recalled Lazarsfeld (quoted in Morrison [1998, 19]).

as a socialist thus animated his academic commitment as a social researcher, and his fascination with methodology drove him to constantly refine his work.

By 1927, when he had completed his Ph.D., Lazarsfeld was working as a teacher of mathematics and physics in a *Gymnasium*, but the advancement of his academic career was frustrated by anti-Semitism at the University of Vienna (Morrison 1998, 22). The ambitious Lazarsfeld was compelled to create a new social research center associated with the Bühler's Institute of Psychology. This became the *Österreichische Wirtschaftspsychologische Forschungsstelle*, the private research institute run by Lazarsfeld over which Karl Bühler presided. The novel structure of the *Forschungsstelle*—which Lazarsfeld would later reproduce in the U.S. at Newark, Princeton, and Columbia—was an institute that was affiliated with a university but had the autonomy to perform "contract" research for outside clients, which were usually commercial concerns. However, Lazarsfeld also worked for political and scholarly organizations like Max Horkheimer's thoroughly Marxist *Institut für Sozialforschung* in Frankfurt (Lazarsfeld 1969, 274–75). Despite its reputation for speculative theory, the *Institut* also sponsored empirical studies from the time Horkheimer assumed the directorship in 1930 (Jay 1973, 24–27). Lazarsfeld thus retained his social-democratic commitments, but he needed a steady source of income to sustain his institute and give it the flexibility to work on projects of his choosing. Moreover, Lazarsfeld's academic interest in the decision-making process and his fascination with methodology trumped whatever uneasiness he might have had with contract work, and commercial projects gave him the opportunity to develop his unique approach to social science research through empirical studies (Stehr 1975, 1). Recalling an early commission from an American market research expert to study consumer motivations in soap buying, Lazarsfeld saw the potential to study decision-making in more manageable context, with fewer complications, than another study he wanted to do on voting: "Such is the origin of my Vienna market research studies: the result of the methodological equivalence of socialist voting and the buying of soap" (Lazarsfeld 1969, 279).

Lazarsfeld made the case to potential commercial clients that his method of investigating consumer motivations—which relied on a systematic tabulation of data derived from directed interviews—could reveal what simple questionnaires could not. He argued that the technological rationalizing of products compelled the "psychological rationalizing of sales" (Lazarsfeld 1932, 11). But the issue of social stratification, of particular concern to Lazarsfeld's cohort of Viennese socialists, remained at the center of his work, and became instrumental in the field of market research. For example, one study developed a profile of the proletarian consumer, whose tastes were different from those of the bourgeois consumer. Working-class consumers, who had access to a narrower range of goods and were ill-informed about them, generally preferred sweet chocolate (and other strong sensory experiences), whereas the upper-class consumer preferred bitter chocolate and generally blander things (Lazarsfeld 1969, 281). These studies allowed Lazarsfeld to hone his method for larger works with a more explicit socialist commitment, such as his book *Jugund und Beruf* (Youth and Occupation), a study of the motivations behind vocational decisions (Zeisel 1979, 12).

The most important of these early works was a study of Marienthal, a depressed Austrian village of 1500 inhabitants that suffered chronic unemployment after the closure of a textile factory.[4] Inspired by the 1929 *Middletown* study by the American sociologists Robert and Helen Lynd, Lazarsfeld set out in 1930 to investigate the use of leisure time by workers, whose unions had recently won a shorter working day. But when he shared his plan with Otto Bauer, leader of the Austrian Social Democratic Party, Lazarsfeld was attacked: how could he study *leisure* time in a period of such high unemployment (Zeisel 1979, 13)? Lazarsfeld subsequently changed course and, along with principal collaborators Zeisel and his first wife Marie Jahoda, and with the financial support from trade unions, commenced the study. *Marienthal* employed diverse methods of empirical research, including field observation, analysis of diaries, examination of organizational archives, and the use of questionnaires and interviews (Barton 1979, 8). To the dismay of its socialist backers, the study revealed that the situation of persistent, widespread unemployment had produced not a revolutionary fervor but rather a general feeling of resignation, apathy, and hopelessness. The depressed residents of Marienthal cared little about politics, did not engage each other in debate, and did not even bother to read the newspaper. According to Jahoda, the interest aroused by the Marienthal study concerned its demonstration of "how a major social problem could be illuminated by social science" in a way that public debate could not. "The public debate produced arguments for two incompatible outcomes of large-scale unemployment: it would create a revolutionary atmosphere or it would create public apathy," wrote Jahoda. "*Marienthal* produced an answer: apathy" (Jahoda 1979, 5). Empirical social research had produced real, discernible knowledge about the motivations, or lack thereof,

---

4 *Die Arbeitlosen von Marienthal* (Leipzig, 1933). The work was finally published in English as *Marienthal, the Sociography of an Unemployed Community* (Jahoda, et. al., 1972).

of a specific social stratum. Charlotte Bühler immediately saw the value of the study and sent Lazarsfeld to the 1932 International Congress of Psychology in Hamburg, where he reported the results of the yet unfinished work (Neurath 1981, 13–14).

The report attracted the attention of the Paris representative of the Rockefeller Foundation, who would offer Lazarsfeld a traveling fellowship to the United States, which he began in September 1933 (Lazarsfeld 1969, 275). Thus it was not his steady work in market research, but rather his exceptional work on unemployment—truer to his socialist inclinations—that brought Lazarsfeld to the U.S. during the Great Depression. The liberal terms of the fellowship granted Lazarsfeld the freedom to pursue whatever projects he wanted, wherever he wanted, and he immediately sought the guidance of his hero Robert Lynd, who would become a friend, colleague, and mentor (Stehr 1975, 2). Lazarsfeld volunteered his help to Lynd, who was studying the effects of unemployment on the middle class. Lynd declined, for fear he would exploit the young man, but he did offer to help him pursue his social research in the U.S. (Neurath 1981, 13–14). With the help of Lynd, Lazarsfeld moved to Washington to begin working on research projects for the Federal Emergency Relief Administration.[5]

Remarkably, Lazarsfeld did not consider himself a sociologist at the time, but rather—given his work for the Bühlers and his interest in human motivations and decision-making—a kind of social psychologist. This disposition lent itself well to market research. Lazarsfeld was drawn to such studies not because he had a particular interest in marketing problems, but mainly because this field could provide him with the opportunity—and, importantly, the money—to practice his empirical methods of investigating motivations. Lazarsfeld seized one such opportunity early on in his fellowship when he learned of a non-profit market research group called the Psychological Corporation (PSC). Lazarsfeld secured a position for himself at PSC, but soon became disillusioned by the banal surveys that the group conducted, mainly to compete with commercial marketing agencies. He proposed projects that would employ his method of motivational research, but they were met with resistance by his behaviorist supervisor (Lazarsfeld 1969, 295). Eventually, though, Lazarsfeld went to work on a number of consumer studies with David Craig of the Retail Research Institute at the University of Pittsburgh, and he

---

5 A Dec. 16, 1933 letter to Lynd, from Hazel K. Stiebeling of the U.S. Department of Agriculture's Bureau of Home Economics, offers to give Lazarsfeld work on a food consumption study. Paul Felix Lazarsfeld Papers, Rare Book and Manuscript Library, Columbia University: Box 2B, folder, 10.

conducted a study for the Market Research Corporation of America on the public's attitude toward advertising. In October of 1934 he published a well-received article in *The Harvard Business Review* on "The Psychological Aspect of Market Research," in which he explained his method of using the statistical analysis of data drawn from interviews to develop a generic profile of the psychological motivations of the typical buyer of a particular commodity (Lazarsfeld 1934).[6] By November of that year—only one year after his arrival in the States—the "portly, bespectacled Dr. Paul F. Lazarsfeld" had caused such a stir that he was profiled in the marketing periodical *Tide*. Lazarsfeld's celebrity in the world of market research was confirmed when he was commissioned to write four chapters for a textbook produced by the American Marketing Association, *The Techniques of Marketing Research*. One of the chapters considered the practice of "depth psychology," which Lazarsfeld cited as the beginning of "motivation research" (Lazarsfeld 1969, 297). Another milestone in this kind of research was the publication, in the summer 1935 issue of *National Marketing Review*, of Lazarsfeld's article, "The Art of asking WHY in Marketing Research." The author disparaged market researchers' exclusive use of "stereotyped" questionnaires, which were unreliable because respondents, whose knowledge of their own motivations may be rather "hazy," inevitably interpreted them differently. Lazarsfeld's methodological innovation was that the consumer's true motivations may be revealed through a persistent, qualitative interview technique—what came to be known as a depth interview—which produced responses that were then classified, tabulated, compared, and quantified (Lazarsfeld 1935).[7]

By this time, fascism and anti-Semitism were on the rise in Austria, where the new Conservative Party had outlawed the Social Democratic Party, terminated Lazarsfeld's teaching position, and imprisoned most of his family, including his parents (Neurath 1981, 14). Given these developments, Lazarsfeld convinced the officers at the Rockefeller Foundation to extend his fellowship for a year, and by the fall of 1935, he had resolved to remain in the United States permanently once he had settled his affairs in Vienna. He had a position ready with Craig at the University of Pittsburgh that earned him a visa, but when that job ultimately fell through, he decided to emigrate anyway, despite the somewhat shaky validity of his papers. "I thus arrived in New

---

6 In a footnote on page 69, Lazarsfeld expressed his gratitude to Charlotte and Karl Bühler, the former for her psychological insight into human development, the latter for his theory of language.

7 David Jenemann describes Lazarsfeld's method as the stabilization of "volatile and fickle subjects" as "consistent and coherent objects along standardized axes" (Jenemann 2007, 5).

York as the classic immigrant, penniless," recalled Lazarsfeld (Lazarsfeld 1969, 304). In fact, however, he had already established many contacts in his new field. His mentor, Lynd, had been applying social research to New Deal government activism in the Consumers Advisory Board (Smith 1994, 148), and he soon helped Lazarsfeld to secure a position as a supervisor of work-relief students. At the University of Newark, Lazarsfeld directed the students' analysis of thousands of questionnaires filled out by unemployed youth for the National Youth Administration, a New Deal program. Such research, like the work at all of Lazarsfeld's institutes, created much-needed jobs and fit well into Lazarsfeld's socialist background, as Morrison notes (Morrison 1998, 57). By the fall of 1936, the enterprising Lazarsfeld had established, with the help of university president Frank Kingdon, a Research Center at Newark on the model of his *Forschungsstelle* in Vienna. Like the *Forschungsstelle*, the Newark Research Center took outside contracts, which covered half of Lazarsfeld's salary and the expenses of the Center. Among the contracts was a study, sponsored by the Works Progress Administration, of Millville, New Jersey, which, like Marienthal, suffered from chronic unemployment as a result of automation in the glass industry (Lazarsfeld 1969, 276, 288–89). As he had in Vienna, Lazarsfeld also did work for Max Horkheimer's Institute of Social Research, which had migrated to Columbia University in 1934 (Jay 1985, 30). Members of the Institute, including Horkheimer and Erich Fromm, had already established friendly relations there with Lazarsfeld's American benefactor Lynd, who encouraged their further collaboration.[8]

Just as Lazarsfeld was settling into his role as director of the center at Newark, John Marshall of the Rockefeller Foundation approached Hadley Cantril, a professor in the social sciences at Princeton, about setting up a radio research project under the auspices of the university. Marshall was an early enthusiast of research into the social effects of mass communications and used his post at the Rockefeller Foundation to direct money to promising projects in this new field. He would later organize the Communications Group, which included Cantril and Lazarsfeld, to bring these scholars together to institutionalize the study of mass media as a new social science (Gary 1999). Though Cantril, who specialized in public opinion, initially expressed little interest in Marshall's proposal to investigate the impact of the powerful new medium of radio on American society, he notified Frank Stanton, a researcher at the

---

8 Robert Lynd, postcard to Paul Lazarsfeld, May 6, 1935. Paul Felix Lazarsfeld Papers: Box 2B, folder, 10. Columbia was the natural home for the Institute, given the contacts its members had nurtured with many Columbia faculty over the years (Jay 1973, 39).

Columbia Broadcasting System (CBS), about the opportunity. "I personally don't give a damn about it since my interests are elsewhere," wrote Cantril to Stanton. "But if you should want it I think we could get something out of Marshall."[9] Lazarsfeld had encountered both Cantril and Stanton while touring the country on his Rockefeller fellowship, and they had him in mind as a possible director of the radio research project, given his experience studying radio at his *Forschungsstelle* in Vienna. Cantril had his doubts, but Lazarsfeld's American savior Lynd once again came to the rescue, convincing Cantril that Lazarsfeld would be perfect for the position. In the summer of 1937, Cantril offered Lazarsfeld the directorship, suggesting that the kind of consumer motivation research that Lazarsfeld had pioneered in Vienna and promoted in American trade journals would be central to the project. Lazarsfeld, attached to his research institutes as "super-personalities," was able to convince Cantril to permit him to direct the project, which became the "Princeton Office of Radio Research," from his center at Newark.[10] The "Princeton" association was thus in name only, and by the summer of 1938, upon the impending collapse of the University of Newark, the project would move to rented space in New York. By the fall of 1939, due partly to a conflict between Cantril and Lazarsfeld, the project finally moved to Columbia University—again with the help of Robert Lynd—where Lazarsfeld joined the sociology faculty and later rechristened his institute as the "Bureau of Applied Social Research" (BASR), the suggestion of associate director Robert Merton, in 1944 (Lazarsfeld 1969, 304–33).

Lazarsfeld's Radio Research project was one of the first centers devoted to the study of mass communications and an innovator in qualitative and quantitative market research methodologies. It was also, importantly, a refuge for émigré scholars from Europe who engaged in diverse modes of social research, but were concerned with the issue of social stratification that had driven Lazarsfeld from his days as a social-democratic activist in Vienna (Neurath 1981, 19). The prodigious output of the radio project included four published volumes and two special issues of the *Journal of Applied Psychology* that documented the myriad analytical modes the researchers used to understand the American public, and its various publics, through the medium of

9 Hadley Cantril, letter to Frank Stanton, Oct. 26, ca. 1936. Frank Stanton Papers, Manuscript Division, Library of Congress, Washington, D.C.: Box 20, folder 11. Stanton later recalled that he was "one of two who brought [Lazarsfeld] to this country," and he took great pleasure in the success of Lazarsfeld, whom he called "one of the giants in the social sciences" (Bartos and Pearson 1977, 28).

10 This is how Lazarsfeld refers to it in his memoir, but it is also commonly referred to as the "Princeton Radio Research Project."

radio. Lazarsfeld's group also collaborated with Max Horkheimer's exiled Institute of Social Research on a special volume of *Studies in Philosophy and Social Science* in 1941 that attempted to bridge the methodological and epistemological divide between humanistic, dialectical critical theory and Lazarsfeld's brand of empirical social research. "It gives us great satisfaction that for the first time some of our ideas have been applied specifically to American subject matters and introduced into the American methodological debate," wrote Horkheimer in the preface. "We feel particularly indebted to Paul F. Lazarsfeld who has taken categories developed by us in a totally different, highly abstract context, and attempted to present them in terms of the concrete desiderata confronting today's social research" (Horkheimer 1941). Such reinterpretation occasionally went in the other direction, as in Frances Holter's article in the radio project's special February 1939 issue of the *Journal of Applied Psychology*. Holter examined materials from the Institute's *Autorität und Familie*, an elaborate empirical study, much like *Marienthal*, concerning the effect of unemployment on parental authority. The study was carried out in Germany before the emigration, with some methodological assistance from Lazarsfeld, and later assembled in 1935 (Jenemann 2007, 7–8). Holter was specifically looking for the role of radio in these families and found it was crucially important to the psychological well-being and status of families that had no money for other entertainments or diversions. When families were forced to sell their radios, the loss was particularly acute for the children, who felt a sharp decline in status because they could no longer invite their friends into their homes to listen to the radio (Holter 1939).

This collaboration between Lazarsfeld and the Institute had begun in Europe, continued at Newark, and became even closer when Lazarsfeld invited Institute associate Theodor Wiesengrund Adorno to direct a study on music in late 1937. At the time, Adorno was living in England, studying at Merton College, Oxford. The Horkheimer group desperately wanted him to join them in the U.S. Lazarsfeld felt indebted to the Institute for their support of his work at the Newark center, and he was intrigued by Adorno's writings on the "contradictory" or critical—in a dialectical sense—role of music in society (Morrison 1998, 107). "I considered it a challenge to see whether I could induce Adorno to try to link his ideas with empirical research," recalled Lazarsfeld (Lazarsfeld 1969, 322). Lazarsfeld sought a "European approach" to the study of music that was more theoretical in its approach to the research problem and more pessimistic in its attitude toward "an instrument of technical progress."[11] He began lobbying Cantril and Stanton early in his tenure at the Radio Research project to bring Adorno on board. "I think that he is another case where a foreigner can be gotten at half the price we would have to pay an American of equal competence," reasoned Lazarsfeld, perhaps in facetious attempt to demonstrate his American-style pragmatism. "I see Frank in conflict between his desire as director to save money and his distrust of foreigners as a native of Ohio."[12] Lazarsfeld's plan was to pair Adorno with an American empiricist, whom he found in the psychologist and jazz musician Gerhard Wiebe, to develop "a convergence of European theory and American empiricism" (Lazarsfeld 1969, 322).

Nonetheless, it would turn out to be a difficult tenure at the radio project for the notoriously stubborn and misanthropic Adorno. Almost immediately after Adorno arrived in February of 1938, Lazarsfeld found himself forced to defend, on intellectual grounds, the odd-looking, "very absent-minded German professor" to the other project directors. Adorno's resolute foreignness made the immigrant Lazarsfeld feel "like a member of the Mayflower Society" (Lazarsfeld 1969, 300–1), and within a year of his arrival Lazarsfeld was complaining to Stanton that the "hard laws of social contacts" were making much trouble for the admittedly brilliant theorist.[13] By the summer of 1939, Lazarsfeld was impelled to write a lengthy personal letter to Adorno, expressing his grave disappointment with his stubborn devotion speculative theory in the context of the empirical Radio Research project (Jay 1973, 222). Indeed, the incompatibility of the American empiricist and the German dialectician was revealed in early meetings between the two. Adorno expressed his impatience with empirical methods, which interested him only insofar as they might help to prove his theories. In discussing a project to investigate audience response to popular music, Adorno asserted that "the reaction of people takes place in a very commodity-like way." He quickly concluded: "Although we are all convinced that this will come out, it will be valuable to check it at any rate."[14] For Adorno, empiricism was a proof of knowledge, not a path to it.

Despite a genuine interest on the part of both parties to bridge the divide

---

11 Letter from Lazarsfeld to Adorno, Nov. 29, 1937 (quoted in Fleck [2011, 176]).

12 Paul Lazarsfeld, memorandum to Hadley Cantril and Frank Stanton, Dec. 15, 1937. Paul Felix Lazarsfeld Papers: Box 3A, folder 7.

13 Paul Lazarsfeld, memorandum to Frank Stanton, Dec. 5, 1938. Paul Felix Lazarsfeld Papers: Box 3A, folder 3.

14 "Results of the Meeting with T. W. A. [Adorno] and G. B. Wiebe, Tuesday and Wednesday, August 30 and 31, 1938." Bureau of Applied Social Research Records, Columbia University, Rare Book & Manuscript Library: Box 1, folder B0070.

between empiricism and critical theory, the fundamental conflict would remain. Morrison, writing on the conflict between Lazarsfeld and Adorno, observes that the latter had a personality "not easily given to recognizing the power of facts where they did not accord with his own suppositions about the world" (Morrison 1978, 337). Lazarsfeld, meanwhile, consciously resisted his own inclinations to empiricism in his desire to incorporate critical theory into his program (Fleck 2011, 104–5). In addition to inviting Frankfurt School scholars like Adorno and Leo Lowenthal to work on his Radio Research project, Lazarsfeld expressed a wish to unite the two modes of inquiry—his own "administrative" research and the opposed "critical" research—in his 1941 contribution to Horkheimer's journal: "The idea of *critical research* is posed against the practice of administrative research, requiring that, prior to and in addition to whatever special purpose is to be served, the general rule of our media of communication in the present social system should be studied" (Lazarsfeld 1941, 9). Lazarsfeld remained so intrigued by critical theory that he would later invite the members of the Institute to join his organization. Horkheimer, however, declined. Horkheimer officially cited his poor health, but he was privately dismissive of the positivistic drift of the sociology at Columbia and Lazarsfeld's willingness to do contract work for big business and the mass-culture industries (Heilbut 1983, 90). However, even though Lazarsfeld felt that "only a very catholic conception of the task of research can lead to valuable results" (Lazarsfeld 1941, 16), he ultimately remained ambivalent about critical theory. While it seemed to have "a core of intellectual integrity," he felt that it was also "foolish and irresponsible," summarizing his feelings as "a mixture of curiosity, interest, respect and irritation" (quoted in Morrison 1978, 352).

That lingering skepticism was certainly shared by many of Lazarsfeld's more pragmatic, American colleagues. Indeed, it was his obsessive empiricism and inclination towards *applied* research that made Lazarsfeld a peculiar sort of émigré and a "doyen of American sociology," according to historian Anthony Heilbut (Heilbut 1983, 77). His champion, the progressive Robert Lynd, was initially attracted to the Frankfurt School members' espousal of social reform and to Lazarsfeld's demonstrated commitment to social democracy. Lynd was also drawn to the Lazarsfeld's devotion to empirical methods, which were partly inspired by his own approach to social research (Wheatland 2005, 181). Nonetheless, Lynd may not have anticipated the degree to which Lazarsfeld would employ sociology in the service of commercial interests, and Heilbut concludes that Lazarsfeld fully sublimated his "revolutionary tendencies" into "marketable use." "Thanks largely to his work," writes Heilbut (1983, 98–99), "mechanical systems of observation could chart everything from voting preferences to tastes in mouthwash and deodorant." This kind of research, which provided a rationale for the administration of consumer tastes and neutered the sociologist's capacity for critical social engagement, was anathema to both Lynd and Adorno. But beyond his distaste for the application of social research in the service of industry, Adorno, despite some initial effort, simply could not resolve empirical methods with critical theory, which was deeply engaged with the problem of commodity fetishism, a Marxian notion that posited the subjective distortion of the consumer's relationship to the product. According to Martin Jay, this was the crux of Adorno's conflict with Lazarsfeld: "Questionnaires or interviews were inadequate because the opinions of the listeners themselves were unreliable" (Jay 1973, 190). Literature scholar David Jenemann defends Adorno on this count, arguing that, if the truth of subjectivity is mutability, then the fixing of subjective elements to a graph amounts to the "liquidation" of subjects, or subject-murder (Jenemann 2007, 6).

Adorno was particularly disturbed by a machine called the "program analyzer" that had been developed by Lazarsfeld and Stanton to measure and quantify audience response to radio programs and commercials. The simple device—by which subjects indicated their approval, disapproval, or indifference to program content in real time through electronic push-buttons—attracted attention in the marketing trade press as a breakthrough in audience research (Creamer and Allen 1941). A promotional brochure hailed the machine as a revolutionary invention in the science of audience analysis. It proclaimed that the program analyzer "points out the straight road from radio advertising to sales," and would help marketers attract the right audience for a particular product, hold their interest, and sustain it through regular listeners.[15] Adorno, mentioned in a 1940 article in *Tide* as an "expert in music research" who had initiated experiments with the gadget, was, in truth, appalled by the thing. Lazarsfeld's empirical methods did nothing to expose reification—the naturalization of historically contingent social phenomena—ultimately reinforcing the artificial norms of capitalist production. After some initial openness to empirical methods, Adorno recoiled from the demand that he produce not insight but information, and resisted by devot-

---

15 "Listen to Your Listeners: How to Improve Your Program with the Lazarsfeld-Stanton Program Analyzer," Consulting Division, Columbia University's Office of Radio Research, ca. 1942. Frank Stanton Papers: Box 20, folder 11.

ing himself mostly to analyzing content, not reception, making broad theoretical suppositions about audience response. Adorno felt that to deny the mass media's standardization, commodification, and "pseudo-individualization" of artistic products would be to submit "reification," or the analysis of society on the basis of its own artificial, institutionalized terms, rather than by critical, historical, and epistemological inquiry—that is, the practice of critical theory (Adorno 1969, 346).

Another Frankfurt School scholar working on Lazarsfeld's Radio Research project, Leo Lowenthal, also chaffed at the reified methods of empirical social research. American social science, he would later write, refused to "enter the sphere of meaning" and, in its obsession with artificially isolated social sectors, tended much too closely to market research and all its associated expediency and tendency to manipulation. "It imagines that horizontal segments constitute its research laboratory," Lowenthal lamented, "and it seems to forget that the only social science laboratories that are properly admissible are historical situations" (Lowenthal 1957, 52). While the pragmatic, mathematically-minded Lazarsfeld quite willingly accepted and worked within the reified categories and social stratifications of empirical research, these stubbornly dialectical critical theorists resisted its inevitable tendency toward marketability as an *applied* science.

Despite their methodological resistance, however, Lowenthal and Adorno did produce substantial work for the project, generally in the field of content analysis—not audience reception—some of which made it to publication. Lowenthal's "Biographies in Popular Magazines," for example, appeared in *Radio Research, 1942–1943,* and was in many ways characteristic of the mass culture criticism practiced by the Frankfurt School. In an argument that bears substantial similarity to the key historical distinction of "inner-direction" and "other-direction" in *The Lonely Crowd* (1950) by David Riesman, an admirer of Lazarsfeld's cohort of social researchers,[16] Lowenthal saw a shift in

---

16 "The concerns of Lazarsfeld and his circle at the Bureau were formative in much of the work that led to *The Lonely Crowd* and *Faces in the Crowd*, including the study of mass media, the panel studies of voting behavior, and the explorations of patterns of personal influence" (Riesman 1979, 211–12). Riesman cited Lowenthal's essay in *The Lonely Crowd* (Riesman 1950a, 243), and in a June 14, 1976 letter to Robert K. Merton, he acknowledged his debt to Lowenthal for the argument in his most famous work: "it is clear from the book how much his famous essay on the shift from idols of production to those of consumption meant as a jumping off place." Robert K. Merton Papers, 1923–2003, Rare Book and Manuscript Library, Columbia University: Box 187, folder "David Riesman, PFL Festshrift." Riesman also referenced the work of Lowenthal, Herzog, and Adorno, and acknowledged his debt to the cohort of European social researchers and critical theorists in a 1950 essay on popular music. "Gifted Europeans," wrote Riesman, "horrified at the alleged vulgarization of taste brought about by industrialization, left-wing critics in the traditions of Marx of Veblen who see popular

the type of figures profiled earlier in the twentieth century, who tended to be "idols of production," as compared to the more contemporary profiles, which featured "idols of consumption." The modern individual appeared no longer as "a center of outwardly bound energies and actions; as an inexhaustible reservoir of initiative and enterprise"—Riesman's "inner-directed" man—but, rather, as an amalgam of consumptive activities. The average man in the contemporary era was much more in line with Riesman's picture of the "other-directed" character, resigned to a life of continual "adjustment to the world through efficiency and industriousness; and adjustment to people by exhibiting amiable and sociable qualities and by repressing all other traits." This would lead to what Lowenthal called a "command psychology," where individuals were not responsible agents but merely the bearers of various "useful or not so useful" character traits projected on them by their social environment (Lowenthal 1944). Lowenthal also contributed to the ongoing discussions of Institute members that led to Adorno and Horkheimer's essay on the "the culture industry" (Jay 1973, 212); this appeared a few years later in *The Dialectic of Enlightenment*, a text that was initially published only in German (*Dialektik der Aufklärung*), failing to enter directly into the American discussion until much later (Jay 1985, 49). Anticipating the argument in that now-famous essay, Lowenthal wrote that, "since the average working day follows a routine which often does not show any change during a life-time, the routine and repetition characteristics of leisure-time activities serve as a kind of justification and glorification of the working day" (Lowenthal 1944, 546).

Adorno—who would come to resent Riesman's "popularization" of the Institute's style of critique (Jay 1985, 49)—ultimately published three works from his time at Lazarsfeld's Office of Radio Research, but only one with its imprimatur: an essay on the "Radio Symphony" that appeared in *Radio Research, 1941*. As Morrison (1978, 343) points out, Adorno's work for Lazarsfeld's organization was alien to the "administrative" work that prevailed there and made its studies so valuable to marketers and mass media corporations. Lazarsfeld sincerely tried to bridge the divide between intellectuals and mass-media producers (Lazarsfeld 1969, 315), but he would regretfully admit that, partly due to his own administrative distractions, his aims fell short. Ultimately, John Marshall, the Rockefeller Foundation officer overseeing Lazarsfeld's radio project, cut off funding for Adorno's music study, which

culture as an antirevolutionary narcotic, high-brows who fear poaching on their preserves by middle-brow 'culture diffusionists'—all these have contributed approaches, and sometimes methods as well, to the present state of research in this field" (Riesman 1950b, 359).

he found aggressively critical, unscientific, and unverifiable (Morrison 1978, 347). Though he respected Adorno's intellect and wavered in his decision (Fleck 2011, 199; Jenemann 2007, 50), Marshall sought to legitimate the field of mass communications research, and the general direction of the Communications Group of scholars was towards behaviorist, empirical research that focused on the *effects* of communications, something Adorno speculated about but did not study empirically. Adorno's work was compelling as social theory, but it was not in line with the public relations objectives of the Rockefeller Foundation (Gary 1999, 87–101).

Although Lazarsfeld's program for "administrative" research was, in many ways, antithetical to the Horkheimer Institute's critical theory, his experience in building institutions was instrumental in supporting the work of the Frankfurt School scholars. Historian Thomas Wheatland credits Lazarsfeld with helping the Horkheimer circle to secure grants from the Jewish Labor Committee and the American Jewish Committee (AJC) for studies on anti-Semitism that were in accord with standard American sociological practices. Moreover, the topic was of urgent concern to the American Jewish community, unlike the somewhat esoteric, academic studies the Institute typically engaged in. These grants, and particularly the one from the AJC, restored the reputation of Horkheimer and Adorno and led to the publication of the Studies in Prejudice series and *The Authoritarian Personality* (Wheatland 2005, 180; Jay 1985, 43–44). The latter study, a collaborative effort of the Berkeley Public Opinion Study Group, contained the famous "F-scale" to measure fascistic personalities. The concept was imagined by Adorno but converted by his colleagues into the quantitative, empirical terms of American sociology. Lazarsfeld was impressed by the project, and he later expressed regret that he had not been able to do the same with Adorno's work while he was with the radio project (Lazarsfeld 1969, 325). The foundational support also freed Adorno and Horkheimer to pursue their more philosophical projects, most notably *The Dialectic of Enlightenment* (Wheatland 2005, 180). Although Horkheimer declined an invitation to formally incorporate the Institute in the sociology department at Columbia, his group did substantially benefit from its association with Lazarsfeld (Jay 1985, 43).

Thus Lazarsfeld's Office of Radio Research, despite its leader's empirical, quantitative proclivities, served as an institutional adjunct to the émigré scholars of the Frankfurt School, and it nurtured their radical critique of mass culture. Although Adorno and other émigré scholars chaffed at Lazarsfeld's positivism, his institutions did much to support the development of a critical, scientific inquiry into mass society. [17] Moreover, some empirical methods were adopted by Horkheimer's Institute, and even Adorno found himself in the awkward position of defending empirical techniques when he later returned to Germany (Jay 1985, 251). Many of the leading figures of the debate over mass culture were either influenced by or directly associated with Lazarsfeld's project. Like Riesman, Dwight Macdonald acknowledged his indebtedness to the early mass culture criticism that came from the Frankfurt scholars working on Lazarsfeld's project (Jay 1985, 48).[18] C. Wright Mills, whose book *White Collar* was central to that discussion, was also indebted to Lazarsfeld's research bureau.[19] Mills, in fact, was recruited to Columbia and to the Bureau of Applied Social Research in 1945 by its directors, Lazarsfeld and Robert Merton. They promptly sent him to Decatur, Illinois to lead the field studies that would provide the basis for Lazarsfeld's seminal work on the "limited" influence of the media, *Personal Influence* (Katz and Lazarsfeld 1955). But that book was published a full ten years after the initial study because of Mills's refusal to conform to Lazarsfeld's quantitative methodology. In the meantime, Mills contemptuously published *White Collar* and *The Power Elite*, which were both based substantially on the Decatur research. Mills's scorn for Lazarsfeld finally boiled over with his publication of *The Sociological Imagination* (Mills 1959), a thinly-veiled attack on Lazarsfeld and what Mills saw as sociology's disturbing tendency towards quantification (Summers 2006).

But early work of the radio project, in particular, broke new ground in the study of media, marketing, and mass culture, with keen attention to social stratification. The first publication from the project, for which it received a special grant from the Rockefeller Foundation, was a study of the hysterical public reaction to the Halloween 1938 radio broadcast of *The War of the*

---

17 Brett Gary notes that émigés Ernst Kris and Hans Speier, who were among the communications scholars associated with Marshall, shared Adorno's aversion to Lazarsfeld's obsession with quantitative methods (Gary 1999, 276).

18 The influence is explicit in Macdonald's essay, "A Theory of Mass Culture," published in the Summer, 1953 issue of the journal *Diogenes*. The author cites Horkheimer and refers to the "brilliant" essay "On Popular Music" by Adorno, and he provides a lengthy summary of Leo Lowenthal's essay on biographies in popular magazines.

19 Robert K. Merton, letter to David Riesman, June 28, 1976. Robert K. Merton Papers: Box 187, folder, "David Riesman, PFL Festshrift." The liberal Riesman, it turned out, had little respect for the slippery methodology of the leftist C. Wright Mills: "Mills really distorted the interviews done for *White Collar*: blinded by his ideology, he saw white collars where there were blue collars, ethnic-colored collars, all sorts of collars." David Riesman, letter to Robert K. Merton, March 29, 1976. Robert K. Merton Papers: Box 187, folder "David Riesman, PFL Festshrift."

Worlds by Orson Welles's Mercury Theatre (Cantril, et al. 1940).[20] Lazarsfeld and Herta Herzog—his second wife and a fellow émigré—resolved that very night to conduct a study of the phenomenon (Fleck 2011, 186). "Such rare occurrences are opportunities for the social scientist to study mass behavior," wrote Cantril, who felt that a study of the widespread panic "should give us insight into the psychology of the common man and, more especially, the psychology of the common man of our times" (Cantril, et al. 1940, vii). The report emphasized that many people, particularly those of lower income and educational levels, had come to rely on the radio rather than newspapers for news, and that the ongoing European crisis had put American listeners on edge. Referring to the study, Lazarsfeld reported that it nicely demonstrated his method of quantifying the data acquired from qualitative interviews conducted in case studies, which functioned to objectify them for general applicability (Lazarsfeld and Robinson 1940, 820). A second volume from 1940, *Radio and the Printed Page*, which was dedicated to Robert and Helen Lynd, anthologized the early work of the project and expanded on the themes of social stratification and the emergence of radio as a mass medium that threatened to overwhelm print (Lazarsfeld 1940). The book contained a study by Herzog on the "Professor Quiz" radio program. The study found that the quiz program served as an outlet for listeners who lacked much formal education to relieve their class resentment towards "college people." "Against the value of a formal education which, in the listener's mind, makes possible a higher social status," concluded Herzog, "the diversified knowledge obtainable through the quiz program raises the listener's position in the eyes of his neighbors" (Herzog 1940, 79).

Perhaps the clearest lineage from the social-democratic heritage of much of the Lazarsfeld cohort to the concerns of project reports may be found in the attention given to market segments, a commercial application of the socialism's critique of class stratification. An article by Lazarsfeld in the first special issue of the *Journal of Applied Psychology*, for example, found that psychological criteria, apart from income, could be just as valid in determining the socioeconomic status of a subject (Lazarsfeld 1939). Similarly, an undated report from the early 1940s, completed as part a broad study of daytime radio serials directed by Herzog, looked at the reaction of respondents to a series of radio commercials. It found that women on lower socio-eco-

---

20 Though Cantril is credited as the principal author, Lazarsfeld later complained that he "had practically nothing to do with it," and his insistence on taking credit for the book led to their falling out and Lazarsfeld's decision to move the project to Columbia (Pasanella 1994, 30).

nomic levels generally preferred highly dramatized, narrative commercials, whereas college-educated women tended to favor descriptive commercials.[21] A 1944 study of wine-drinking habits found that, while both upper-class and working-class consumers enjoyed wine as an "escape," their psychological motivations were entirely different. Working-class drinkers desired wine for its "pep and stimulation," as an exciting diversion from monotony, whereas high-income drinkers enjoyed it as an aid to relaxation (Watson 1944). A cover letter from Lazarsfeld to the company that had commissioned the report noted that higher income groups tend to prefer more subdued sensations, like dry rather than sweet wines. "Sweet rather than bitter chocolate, strongly smelling flower perfumes, louder colors are better liked in the lower income groups," observed Lazarsfeld. "This should give leads as to what one should stress in advertising in magazines which are known to reach different social strata."[22] Lazarsfeld frequently cited this anecdote, from his early market studies in Vienna, suggesting a lasting sensitivity to the variable tastes, desires, and motivations of different social strata (Lazarsfeld 1959).

The project's concern for social stratification was also evident in its fourth published volume, *Radio Research, 1942–1943*, which contained a multifaceted study directed by Herzog on listeners of daytime radio serials, a.k.a., "soap operas," an allusion to their commercial sponsors. The study included an analysis of the narrative content of the programs by Rudolf Arnheim, in which the author argued that, due to the attentiveness with which the commercial producers of the serials met the desires of their intended market, much could be revealed about that audience through the substance of the programs. Arnheim found the working classes fully unrepresented by the protagonists of the serials he analyzed. However, he also found that personal qualities—accessible to all and independent of political economy— were means by which social inequality was countered. Moreover, the problems that the principal characters encountered were caused not by social, economic, or political conditions, but rather by *individuals*, and particularly by *male* individuals. Arnheim speculated that these vaguely ill but incomprehensible social forces unconsciously took human shape in unambiguously "bad" villains whose actual position in the social context was never interro-

---

21 "Preliminary Test of Six Kolynos Commercials," ca. 1942. Bureau of Applied Social Research Records: Box 2.

22 "Wine Drinking—Motives, Kinds and Conditions: Interim Report Number III," BASR, March 27, 1944. Bureau of Applied Social Research Records: Box 113.

gated. Any dissatisfaction present in the protagonist, with whom the listener identified, did not produce a desire for improvement or reformation, but was instead "*drained off by substitute gratification*" (Arnheim 1944, 78).

Another study in the volume, "On the Psychology of Radio Commercials," was written by Ernest Dichter, later to become famous as the main proponent of "motivation research," which he practiced as a quasi-Freudian, psycho-analytic probe into the consumer unconscious through a series of "depth" interviews with willing subjects. Dichter was one of the more qualitatively-inclined market researchers affiliated with the project who came from the same circle of Viennese social psychologists that produced Lazarsfeld. Like Lazarsfeld, Dichter had studied under Charlotte Bühler at the University of Vienna. Dichter took a statistics course taught by Lazarsfeld and worked for his *Forschungsstelle*, conducting studies of milk drinking habits. But unlike Lazarsfeld, Dichter was largely apolitical aside from a tentative youthful flirtation with socialism—more properly, with young and attractive socialists. He resented being arrested by Austrian fascists while working for Lazarsfeld's *Forschungsstelle*, which had been a center of social-democratic activities. Dichter recalled that, after the raid, the papers reported, not incorrectly, that "market research and public opinion research had been used to cleverly disguise the subversive socialist activities of the underground" (Dichter 1979, 17). However, his interest in market research stemmed not from its political application, methodological opportunities, or concern with social stratification. Dichter was drawn to the business of marketing and consumerism out of revulsion at his own childhood poverty and a desire to evangelize his personal philosophy of hedonism which, he felt, was not only good for the individual, but good for modern capitalism (Dichter 1960). His main motivation was not a desire for socialism, but rather a longing to emulate his rich uncle who had given him a job in his department store and encouraged his early interest in marketing (Dichter 1979, 56). Because of this early experience in the commercial world, Dichter claimed, he was never interested in an academic career and always maintained a hostile attitude toward pure theory that had no practical application (Kreuzer 2007, 23–24).

Despite their differences, the two Viennese market researchers had regular meetings and correspondence, traveled in the same circle of émigré intellectuals and social researchers and were close friends. However, it is evident from Dichter's diaries that he constantly felt slighted by Lazarsfeld, with Lazarsfeld remaining deeply skeptical of Dichter's strictly qualitative, quasi-mystical, and unscientific approach to consumer motivations.[23] Moreover, Lazarsfeld felt—incorrectly, as it turned out—that Dichter's European style and methods would be totally rejected in positivistic America. "Americans don't understand psychology; all they believe in are figures and statistics," Lazarsfeld advised the new immigrant, as recalled by Dichter. "If there are percentage points behind a nonsensical statement, they're happy" (Bartos and Pearson 1977, 3). Lazarsfeld, of course, recognized he could use the American "worship of percentages" (Dichter 1979, 45–46), and his early embrace by both social scientists and marketers in the U.S. is a testament to the veracity of this observation. Dichter's success in business may have had more to do with his entrepreneurial spirit, and his talent for self-promotion, than the potential application of his ideas; in fact, the very mystery of his method probably enhanced his allure.

While his Viennese colleagues Herta Herzog and Hans Zeisel remained employed by advertising firms, and while Lazarsfeld kept his institutes affiliated with universities, Dichter's lack of patience with institutional constraints and the demands of quantitative research inspired him to sell himself as a "psychological" marketing consultant with a unique perspective. Early on, Dichter managed to acquire contracts for studies on *Esquire* magazine, Proctor and Gamble's Ivory soap, and Chrysler's Plymouth line. But in his first years in the U.S. he often struggled to find work, and to keep work, as he generally refused to submit to the demands of his employers, and he was constantly worried about being fired.[24] Dichter generally spurned the quantitative methodology of Lazarsfeld, instead applying—somewhat crudely—his own brand of *Gestalt*, or "image," theory to the study of consumer motivation. While occasionally working for Lazarsfeld's project and sometimes taking patients for analysis, Dichter consulted for an advertising agency and a market research firm, and for several years worked as a researcher for Stanton at CBS, a position he secured with the help of Lazarsfeld (Dichter 1979, 44). The job introduced him to Leo Lowenthal, whom he found "not americanized enough" to do him "any good," though he hoped to somehow exploit his connection with Horkheimer's Institute of Social Research. Dichter, who desperately wanted to fit into the American scene and lose his foreignness,

---

23 Ernest Dichter Papers, Hagley Museum and Library, Wilmington, Delaware: Box 161, folders "Diary – 1942" and "Diary, 1943–1944."

24 Ernest Dichter Papers: Box 161, folders "Diary – 1942" and "Diary, 1943–1944."

had better relations with Zeisel. However, he also found him to be "a silly guy, completely unassimilated."[25]

Along with his CBS colleague Oscar Katz, Dichter conducted a number of studies on the new medium of television and the composition of its audiences, which were reported in a series of articles, "Studies in Television," in the advertising trade periodical *Tide* in 1945. Dichter and Katz described their efforts to understand the desires and motivations of Americans as they encountered the new medium. Its commercial applications were immediately apparent, and the researchers' respondents felt that television, with its moving pictures beamed right into the home, would be particularly useful in showing them how to do things, "how to become beautiful, how to play the piano, how to make a dress, how to use cosmetics." The authors noted that advertisers may take advantage of this desire with "how-to-do" commercials." "Audience participation" programs were another venue ripe for commercial exploitation, because of television's spontaneity and "magic quality" to transport viewers to the scene of the action. Dichter and Katz also warned producers that, in contrast to radio, television was not seen as a "background activity." To avoid inducing guilt feelings in the homemaker, the researchers recommended programs and commercials that "will help viewers in their housework or in their shopping" so that women had a legitimate excuse to tune in to daytime programming. *Immediacy* was another important quality of television, because it allowed it to "come closer to the normal buying-selling situation than any other form of advertising." While radio had been the most important medium for commercial market research, it was clear that television had the potential to displace it.

Dichter's position at CBS during the war years was always very tenuous—he was ultimately let go—and he constantly dreamed of starting his own firm, which he eventually did in 1946. Methodological differences aside, Dichter's association with Lazarsfeld is significant in terms of the model the latter established for building institutions and doing commercial work for paying clients. But where Lazarsfeld's socialist background translated into a commitment to developing a scientific methodology to interpret social stratification, Dichter's childhood poverty produced an absolute rejection of austerity and a total embrace of the affluent society. "We have to learn to accept the morality of the good life," Dichter later wrote with the fervor of an evangelical, capitalistic hedonist. "We must use the modern techniques of motivational think-

---

25 Ernest Dichter Papers: Box 161, folder "Diary, 1943–1944."

ing and social science to make people constructively discontented by chasing them out of the false paradise of knowledgeless animal happiness into the real paradise of change and progress" (Dichter 1960, 263–64). Lazarsfeld's political background and academic training provided him with the intellectual perspective to analyze social stratification in a way that was useful to marketers, and Dichter's desire to preach the moral goodness of personal indulgence—a reaction to repressive, puritanical austerity—motivated his own desire to probe the consumer unconscious in the service of business.

III

While Dichter represented the ultimate embrace of the capitalistic ethos, and Adorno and Lowenthal represented the ultimate rejection of capitalistic reification, they were all indebted to the institutional framework provided by Lazarsfeld, whose fundamental social-democratic commitments were translated into highly instrumental modes of market research in the United States. These émigré scholars brought to the U.S. a Continental commitment to social inquiry and a penetrating understanding of human motivations that they integrated, willingly or begrudgingly, with the applied science of market research. The Frankfurt School critique of mass media and mass culture, a profoundly anti-capitalist enterprise, had its origins in Lazarsfeld's Rockefeller-funded radio project. Dichter's celebration of hedonism, meanwhile, ultimately took its form as a contract firm on the model of Lazarsfeld's research institutes but without the legitimation of a university affiliation. The divergent paths taken by Lazarsfeld's professional associates and intellectual comrades suggest a dynamic, dialectical relationship of socialist and capitalist ideas that belies the antithetical relationship of these economic models. Socialism's critique of capitalism emphasized the severity of social stratification, a critical insight that was vigorously applied—or exploited—by marketers and their research consultants.

References

Adorno, T. W. 1941. "The Radio Symphony: An Experiment in Theory." In *Radio Research, 1941*, edited by Paul F. Lazarsfeld and Frank N. Stanton, 110–39. New York: Duell, Sloan and Pearce.

———. 1969. "Scientific Experiences of a European Scholar in America." Translated by Donald Fleming. In *The Intellectual Migration: Europe and America, 1930–1960*, edited by Donald Fleming and Bernard Bailyn. Cambridge, MA: Harvard University Press.

Arnheim, R. 1944. "The World of the Daytime Serial." In *Radio Research, 1942–1943*, edited by Paul F. Lazarsfeld and Frank N. Stanton, 34–85. New York: Essential Books.

Barton, A. H. 1979. "Paul Lazarsfeld and the Invention of the University-Based Applied Social Research Institute." March 13. Robert K. Merton Papers, 1923–2003, Rare Book and Manuscript Library, Columbia University: Box 185, folder 6.

Bartos, R., and A. S. Pearson. 1977. "The Founding Fathers of Advertising Research." *Journal of Advertising Research* 17, no. 3.

Cantril, H., with H. Gaudet and H. Herzog. 1940. *The Invasion from Mars: A Study in the Psychology of Panic with the Complete Script of the Famous Orson Welles Broadcast*. Princeton, NJ: Princeton University Press.

Creamer, J., and G. H. Allen. 1941. "Ups and Downs in Audience Interest." *Advertising & Selling*, July.

Dichter, E. 1960. *The Strategy of Desire*. Garden City, NY: Doubleday & Company, Inc.

———. 1979. *Getting Motivated: The Secret behind Individual Motivations by the Man Who Was Not Afraid to Ask "Why?"* New York: Pergamon Press.

Fleck, C. 2011. *A Transatlantic History of the Social Sciences: Robber Barons, the Third Reich and the Invention of Empirical Social Research*. Translated by Hella Beister. London: Bloomsbury Academic.

Fleming, D., and B. Bailyn, eds. 1969. *The Intellectual Migration: Europe and America, 1930–1960*. Cambridge, MA: Harvard University Press.

Gary, B. 1999. *The Nervous Liberals: Propaganda Anxieties from World War I to the Cold War*. New York: Columbia University Press.

Heilbut, A. 1983. *Exiled in Paradise: German Refugee Artists and Intellectuals in America, from the 1930s to the Present*. New York: Viking Press.

Herzog, H. 1940. "Professor Quiz—A Gratification Study." In *Radio and the Printed Page: An Introduction to the Study of Radio and Its Role in the Communi-*

cation of Ideas, edited by Paul F. Lazarsfeld, 64–93. New York: Duell, Sloan and Pearce.

Holter, F. 1939. "Radio among the Unemployed." *Journal of Applied Psychology* 23: 163–69.

Horkheimer, M. 1941. "Preface." *Studies in Philosophy and Social Science* 9.

Jahoda, M. 1979. "PFL: Hedgehog or Fox?" In *Qualitative and Quantitative Social Research: Papers in Honor of Paul F. Lazarsfeld*, edited by Robert K. Merton, James S. Coleman, and Peter H. Rossi, 10–15. New York: The Free Press.

Jay, M. 1973. *The Dialectical Imagination: A History of the Frankfurt School and the Institute of Social Research.* Boston: Little, Brown, and Company.

———. 1985. *Permanent Exiles: Essays on the Intellectual Migration from Germany to America.* New York: Columbia University Press.

Jenemann, David. 2007. *Adorno in America.* Minneapolis: University of Minnesota Press.

Katz, E., and P. F. Lazarsfeld. 1955. *Personal Influence: The Part Played by People in the Flow of Mass Communications.* Glencoe: The Free Press.

Kreuzer, F. 2007. "THE SECRET FREUDIAN: Ernest Dichter as a Witness of His Work." In *A Tiger in the Tank: Ernest Dichter, An Austrian Advertising Guru*, edited by Franz Kreuzer et al. Translated by Lars Hennig. Riverside, California: Ariadne Press.

Lazarsfeld, P. F. 1932. "New Ways of Investigating Markets" (translation of *Neue Weze der Marktferschung*). Presentation to the meeting of the "Mercantile Advertising Committee" at the Chamber of Commerce and Industry in Berlin, October. Paul Felix Lazarsfeld Collection, Rare Book and Manuscript Library, Columbia University: Box 175, folder 9.

———. 1934. "The Psychological Aspect of Market Research." *Harvard Business Review* 13: 54–71.

———. 1935. "The Art of Asking WHY in Marketing Research: Three Principles Underlying the Formulation of Questionnaires." *National Marketing Review* 1: 26–38.

———. 1939. "Interchangeability of Indices in the Measurement of Economic Influences." *Journal of Applied Psychology* 23: 33–45.

———. 1940. *Radio and the Printed Page: An Introduction to the Study of Radio and Its Role in the Communication of Ideas.* New York: Duell, Sloan and Pearce.

———. 1941. "Remarks on Administrative and Critical Communications Research." *Studies in Philosophy and Social Science* 9: 2–16.

———. 1959. "Sociological Reflections on Business: Consumers and Managers." In *Social Science Research on Business: Product and Potential*, edited by

Robert A. Dahl, Mason Haire, and Paul F. Lazarsfeld. New York: Columbia University Press.

————. 1969. "An Episode in the History of Social Research: A Memoir." In *The Intellectual Migration: Europe and America, 1930–1960*, edited by Donald Fleming and Bernard Bailyn. Cambridge, MA: Harvard University Press.

Lazarsfeld, P. F., and W. S. Robinson. 1940. "The Quantification of Case Studies." *Journal of Applied Psychology* 24: 817–25.

Lazarsfeld, P. F., and F. N. Stanton. 1941. *Radio Research, 1941*. New York: Duell, Sloan and Pearce.

Lazarsfeld, P. F., and F. N. Stanton, eds. 1944. *Radio Research, 1942–1943*. New York: Essential Books.

Lowenthal, L. 1944. "Biographies in Popular Magazines." In *Radio Research, 1942-1943*, edited by Paul F. Lazarsfeld and Frank N. Stanton, 507–48. New York: Essential Books.

————. 1957. "Historical Perspectives of Popular Culture." In *Mass Culture: The Popular Arts in America*, edited by Bernard Rosenberg and David Manning White. Glencoe, IL: The Free Press.

Mills, C. W. 1959. *The Sociological Imagination*. New York: Oxford University Press.

Morrison, D. 1978. "Kultur and Culture: The Case of Theodor W. Adorno and Paul Lazarsfeld." *Social Research* 45: 331–55.

————. 1988. "The Transference of Experience and the Impact of Ideas: Paul Lazarsfeld and Mass Communications Research." *Communications*: 185–209.

————. 1998. *The Search for a Method: Focus Groups and the Development of Mass Communication Research*. Luton, UK: University of Luton Press.

Neurath, P. 1981. "Paul F. Lazarsfeld and the Institutionalization of Empirical Social Research." Paper given before a joint session of the Columbia University Seminars on Content and Method of the Social Sciences and Mathematical Methods in the Social Sciences, November 11, 1981. Robert K. Merton Papers, 1923–2003, Rare Book and Manuscript Library, Columbia University: Box 185, folder 7.

Pasanella, A. K. 1994. "The Mind Traveller: A Guide to Paul F. Lazarsfeld's Communication Research Papers." The Freedom Forum Media Studies Center, Columbia University. Robert K. Merton Papers, 1923–2003: Box 444, folder 5.

Riesman, D., with R. Denney and N. Glazer. 1950a. *The Lonely Crowd: A Study of the Changing American Character*. New Haven: Yale University Press.

Riesman, D. 1950b. "Listening to Popular Music." *American Quarterly* 2: 359–71.

————. 1979. "Ethical and Practical Dilemmas of Fieldwork in Academic Set-tings: A Personal Memoir." In *Qualitative and Quantitative Social Research: Papers in Honor of Paul F. Lazarsfeld,* edited by Robert K. Merton, James S. Coleman, and Peter H. Rossi, 210–31. New York: The Free Press.

Smith, M. C. 1994. *Social Science in the Crucible: The American Debate Over Objec-tivity and Purpose, 1918–1941.* Durham, NC: Duke University Press.

Simonson, P., and G. Weimann. 2003. "Critical Research at Columbia: Lazars-feld's and Merton's 'Mass Communication, Popular Taste, and Organized Social Action.'" In *Canonic Texts in Media Research: Are There Any? Should There Be? How About These?* edited by Elihu Katz, John Durham Peters, Tamar Liebes, and Avril Orloff. Cambridge, UK: Polity Press.

Stehr, N. ca. 1975. "Conversation with P. F. Lazarsfeld." Transcript of inter-view. Robert K. Merton Papers, 1923–2003, Rare Book and Manuscript Library, Columbia University: Box 185, folder 7.

Summers, J. H. 2006. "Perpetual Revelations: C. Wright Mills and Paul Lazars-feld." *Annals of the American Academy of Political and Social Science* 608: 25–40.

Watson, G. 1944. "A Socio-Psychological Study of Wine Drinking: Final Sum-mary Report," Office of Radio Research, Consulting Division, April 7. Bureau of Applied Social Research Records, Rare Book and Manuscript Library, Columbia University: Box 113.

Wheatland, Thomas. 2005. "Not-Such-Odd Couples: Paul Lazarsfeld and the Horkheimer Circle on Morningside Heights." In *Exile, Science, and Bildung: The Contested Legacies of German Emigre Intellectuals,* edited by David Kettler and Gerhard Lauer. New York: Palgrave Macmillan.

Zeisel, H. 1979. "The Vienna Years." In *Qualitative and Quantitative Social Research: Papers in Honor of Paul F. Lazarsfeld,* edited by Robert K. Merton, James S. Coleman, and Peter H. Rossi, 10–15. New York: The Free Press.

Open Article

Darnton's Cats
Text or Reality?

Eivind Engebretsen[1]

Abstract

Although researchers within the history of mentalities have highlighted the importance of text and interpretation, few have accorded the text status as the historian's real object of study. It is behind the text—in "reality"—that most historians define their object. The text is not an integral part of the ontology of the history of mentalities, i.e., the definition of reality upon which the history of mentalities is built. This paper claims that the linguistic turn has been reductively interpreted by historians as a question of epistemology and it discusses the analytical implications of dealing with the text as an integral part of history of mentalities' ontology. The article first describes Derrida's text ontology and argues that the history of mentalities can learn more from this approach. Secondly, this perspective is concretized through the analysis of a modern classic within the field—Robert Darnton's study of the cat massacre. Unlike Darnton, who uses the "little narrative" about a cat massacre as input to describe a cultural grammar behind the text, this article emphasizes the study of the text itself as a venue for local cultural negotiations. This leads to a critique of Darnton's conclusions: the story of the cat massacre does not give grounds to see the cat as a symbol of greater distance between master and journeymen. The text is a stage for complex intertextual references in which master and journeymen are both played off against each other and united through their relations to cats and the cat's symbolic significance.

In 1984, Robert Darnton published *The Great Cat Massacre and Other Episodes in French Cultural History*. The book has now achieved status as a classic and has been translated into seventeen languages. One of the reasons for the book's success is its innovative contribution to historical research. The book is situated within a historiographic tradition often referred to as the history of mentalities (*histoire des mentalités*). The history of mentalities dif-

---

1 Eivind Engebretsen is professor of philosophy and history of science in the Department of Health Science, University of Olso.

fers from traditional history of ideas, which has been concentrated on elite thinking, by focusing on the mental universe of ordinary people. Originally, the history of mentalities was associated with French historians and the journal *Les Annales*. However, it has gradually developed into an international research tradition. Robert Darnton, Carlo Ginzburg and Peter Burke are some of its main representatives.

In line with this tradition, ordinary thought is the focus of Darnton's studies. He is, however, not interested in ideas that are today considered ordinary. Inspired by modern anthropology (Clifford Geertz in particular), Darnton makes the most opaque and alien aspects of past thinking into the object of his study. It is exactly when we cannot get a proverb, or a joke, or a ritual, or a poem that we know that we are on to something. Darnton (1984, 5) claims that it is this "methodology of surprise" that has guided the selection of texts for his study. Darnton (1984, 5) writes that he has selected documents that "cannot be taken to typify eighteenth-century thought but that provide ways of entering into it." More precisely, his material consists of an early version of "Little Red Riding Hood," a story about a cat massacre, a description of a city and a file kept by a police inspector. Darnton thus differs from former generations of the so called *Annales* school that operated with abundant and often quantified empirical data. In line with a third generation of *Annales* researchers, Darnton's method is case-based and micro-oriented. He is interested in signs and symbols rather than events or ideas and can therefore be seen as a representative of the so called "linguistic turn" within the history of mentalities. More precisely he is concerned with the interpretations of stories, of small narratives. According to Darnton, "small narratives" may, however, bring us on the trail of something bigger—namely a cultural grammar that characterized seventeenth-century France.

Although Darnton's book has been praised for its originality, it also generated debate. When the book was first published it provoked discussion about the significance of text and reading in historical research which resulted in several articles in the *Journal of Modern History* in the late 1980s (Chartier 1985; Fernandez 1988; LaCapra 1988). The intellectual historians, Roger Chartier and Dominick LaCapra, were among the most important contributors to the debate. Although both Chartier and LaCapra recognize Darnton's innovative contribution and applaud his interest in signs and symbols, they criticize him for underestimating the role of text and textuality. From different angles they both object to Darnton's portraying of the relationship between text and historical reality as a one to one relationship. Thus, they both criticize him for not having taken the linguistic turn far enough. According to Chartier, Darnton sees any text as an image of a social reality without taking into account its specific task and function. The question of whether the text can be read as a description of social conditions depends on the text's intention, Chartier (1985, 692) claims. LaCapra, for his part, emphasizes how Darnton in his pursuit of the most alien aspects of the past uses a reading strategy that implies transforming the alien into the known by fitting it into a dense symbol system, a cultural grammar (LaCapra 1988, 104). He points out that meaning cannot be abstracted from the text—at least not as unproblematically as Darnton claims—and that the hermeneutic circle cannot be definitely closed (LaCapra 1988,112) .

The sharpest critique of Darnton came however some years later in an article written by Harold Mah in *History Workshop Journal* (1991). Through a rereading of the case of the cat massacre, Mah argues that Darnton simplifies the text when he interprets it as a social revolution before the Revolution. "The text contains conflicting narrative registers—it tries over and over again to write romances of riot, rebellion, and emancipation. But each of these is cancelled out, the narrative movement toward liberation is aborted or swerves back to obedience" (Mah 1999, 15). The revolt is therefore only temporary and submits eventually to consensus and order.

On a more fundamental level, Mah's critique differs from that of Chartier and LaCapra in that he is less concerned with the epistemological limits of Darnton's material than its unexploited potential. While Chartier and LaCapra thinks that Darnton draws too much from his material, Mah thinks that he draws too little from it. Darnton is supressing the text, Mah claims.

Despite these differences all three critiques have one thing in common: Darnton's *approach* is questioned. Darnton's choice of study object, however—social reality—is not contested. Both Chartier and LaCapra emphasize the fact that they do not dispute the connection drawn between text and social reality as such, but rather Darnton's way of connecting them (Chartier 1985, 692; LaCapra 1988, 112). Mah criticizes Darnton for simplifying the text. However, he doesn't challenge the assumption that it is behind the text—in reality—that history unfolds. He himself turns to political contexts to explain Darnton's text but only a slightly different context than the one highlighted by Darnton: "the self-neutralizing play of signifiers, the direct historical context, the conclusions of the editor, the putative royal reader—all these point to a text contaminated by immediate political concerns and submission to authority; none of these is considered by Darnton" (Mah 1999, 16). Darnton's critics argue a more self reflective and nuanced approach to texts. However, the text is still kept on the outside of their definition of historical reality. One might say that the linguistic turn they represent is only epistemological, not ontological.

I consider the Darnton debate as a good place to address the more general problem of the ontology of historical studies after the linguistic turn. Although the linguistic turn has had a significant impact on the historiographical debate, the question of ontology has been surprisingly little debated. The debate has to a large extent been restricted to the epistemological question of how to reach historical truth.[2] In a time when the linguistic turn is met with criticism, I find it particularly opportune to stress that it is a quite reductive understanding of this so called turn that has been adopted by historians and that it is the same reductive understanding that today is met with criticism (Kirby 2006; Mortimer 2008). There are other—and in my opinion more important—aspects of the linguistic turn and its consequences for historiography that still need to be debated. By reopening the debate about Darnton, I also wish to address the broader question of how to define the historian's research object, i.e., historical reality after the linguistic turn.

This will be done through a two-step approach. First I will discuss Jacques Derrida's text concept and how this relates to the question of historical reality. I will argue that Derrida lays the foundation for a text ontology that has potential implications for the history of mentalities. Derrida's view on these matters is in my opinion never more clearly stated than in his famous debate with Foucault on Descartes, and I will to a large extent use Derrida's critique of Foucault as basis for my discussion. Second, I will specify Derrida's theoretical assumptions by returning to the discussion about Darnton. Based on Derrida's conception of text, I will take the criticism of Chartier, LaCapra, and Mah a step further by also questioning Darnton's ontology. Could Darnton's historical research object be defined differently? What would be the analytical consequences of treating Darnton's "little narrative" not only as the means of his study but also as its final end?

In order to understand Derrida's text concept and its underlying ontological assumptions that will guide my answers to the questions above, we first need to take a closer look at Derrida's famous critique of Foucault in the essay "Cogito et l'histoire de la folie" from *L'Ecriture et la différence* (1967).

---

2 Along with Darnton and his critics some of the most prominent debaters of these questions have been Hayden White (1973), Keith Jenkins (1991, 1997, 1999), Alun Munslow (1997), Perez Zagorin (1999, 1–24), Robert F. Berkhofe (1995), and Frank Ankersmit (Ankersmit and Hans Kellner 1995)

I will argue that on a principle level, Derrida's discussion is based on a different understanding of historical research objects than Foucault's. Yet, as often with Derrida, the immediate topic of his essay is not general theoretical questions but the reading of a specific text, in this case Descartes's *Metaphysical Meditations*. To capture Derrida's underlying theoretical assumptions we therefore need to take a brief look at Derrida's reading of Descartes.

The Debate about the Cogito

The point of departure of Derrida's critique is Foucault's interpretation of Descartes in *History of Madness* (1961/1972). In his "First Meditation," Descartes (2006) mentions three ways in which the senses can deceive us: sense deception, madness and dream. Foucault claims that Descartes treats madness differently than the other two examples of deception. The possibility that he could be mad is dismissed as a possibility already at the outset, because it is impossible to think and at the same time be insane. Thus Descartes draws a distinction between madness and thought—thought and madness are mutually exclusive concepts—and thereby, according to Foucault, Descartes excludes madness from Cogito. With this background, Foucault reads Descartes's work as a statement within a larger dialogue or discourse in the seventeenth century in which distinctions between reason and madness were drawn (Derrida 1967, 74; Foucault 1972).

According to Derrida, the problem with Foucault's reading is that Foucault does not take into account what kind of text he has to do with: the madness example should be read as part of a hyperbolic argument in which one example over-bids the other by being more radical, more comprehensive. Derrida (1967, 78) emphasizes that the expression *sed forte*, which opens the section on madness, not only must be read as a "but," but as a "but .... perhaps." Descartes (2008, 74) writes, "But it may be said, *perhaps*, that, although the senses occasionally mislead us respecting minute objects, and such as are so far removed from us as to be beyond the reach of close observation, there are yet many other of their informations (presentations), of the truth of which it is manifestly impossible to doubt." "Perhaps" transforms the counter-argument into a potential counter-argument, Derrida argues: "We can see how the pedagogical and rhetorical meaning of *sed forte* governs the entire paragraph. It is the "perhaps" of a fake argument" (Derrida 1967, 78, my translation). The objection is a hypothetical objection from a critical listener.

According to Derrida, this difference between "but" and "but ... perhaps" is crucial for understanding the role of madness in relation to the examples of deception mentioned in the foregoing and in the subsequent section. Dream, the example that is given afterwards, does not replace the madness example but exceeds it, according to Derrida. Descartes tries to convince his reader through a more radical example. In the dream section, Descartes opens again for the possibility that his senses are false illusions, which the critical listener in the previous paragraph rejected as "madness." According to Derrida, Descartes does not exclude the possibility that he may be crazy, as Foucault claims; rather he just pretends that he does. Descartes (1967, 75) allows his implied critical reader to advance his counter-arguments, for in the next turn to refute them through a more comprehensive and radical example, through a hyperbole. It is through hyperbolic demonstration that Descartes arrives at his famous Cogito experience: even if the senses were deceiving me, even though I were insane, yes, even worse, even if I were dreaming, those are thoughts that confirm my existence—I think therefore I am. According to Derrida, the fundamental audacity of the Cogito lies in the hyperbole: it is a quest for a foundation of knowledge that is prior to all classification and dualism. Unlike Foucault, Derrida believes that madness is not enclosed in a sphere outside Cogito, but that it is included. Cogito, ergo sum, either I'm insane or not (Derrida 1967, 86, see also Schaanning 1997).

That said, Derrida also thinks Descartes draws a distinction between reason and madness. This occurs, however, at a much later stage of the argument than Foucault claims. It is only when Descartes turns to God and tries to prove His existence that he "rationalizes" Cogito. Although Cogito remains open to the possibility of madness, God is used as an alibi for the mental sanity of the subject. When Descartes has demonstrated that God exists and that He doesn't deceive, he may also conclude that everything that "I" recognize is necessarily true.

Derrida still disagrees with Foucault: Descartes's exclusion of madness is not new, as Foucault claims, but very old. The argument is based on a rhetorical tool—the proof of God's existence and goodness which have roots in scholasticism (Derrida 1967, 90). Derrida thus questions Foucault's assumption that the distinction between reason and madness is first drawn in Descartes's time. The dichotomy is much older. In Descartes's text, it is the confinement of madness that makes up the hegemonic position that Descartes argues against: it is an established rather than an innovative position. But more importantly, Descartes's text also contains a different voice, a hyperbole, a voice that transcends this dichotomy. That is, as Derrida sees it, what is new in

Descartes's project. The break with tradition lies in the hyperbolic Cogito not in the confinement of madness.

Derrida's No-Outside-Text Ontology

Derrida's critique of Foucault and his own reading of Descartes is based on a premise that he summarizes in his main work *De la grammatologie*: "Il n'y a pas de hors-texte"—"There is no outside-text (Derrida 1969, 227)." As is so often the case with Derrida, the statement is ambiguous. First it means that a text does not rest on a social reality outside the text, but has an independent existence. It is in the text that history takes place, not on the outside. Inside Descartes's text, for example, there are cultural meetings between different writing traditions in the form of hyperbolic argumentation and scholastic theosophical evidence. Even though the text draws on diverse traditions, the actual meeting takes place *in* Descartes's text, not outside it. Second, Derrida's statement points to the fact that *no texts are complete.* The text's meaning cannot be framed, concluded or enclosed in one interpretation. This applies to both individual texts and discourses or systems of meaning such as the seventeenth century debate on madness. The parameters of the interpretation cannot be defined by two cardboard covers, or by a specific year or a specific culture—because the text will not allow itself to be limited. Neither the text nor its respective contexts are clear cut but refer the reader onwards to new texts and contexts. Neither seventeenth-century socio-political discourse, hyperbolic argumentation or scholastic theosophical evidence provide the key to a final interpretation of Descartes. All the contexts we read into the text are texts that must themselves be interpreted. The meaning of a text is thus always ambiguous: the text holds a large (if not unlimited) meaning potential. There is no way to settle the continuous struggle of signification going on within a text. There is no fixed point. Every text is therefore deconstructible.

This leads on to a third meaning of Derrida's statement. In French, the word *hors-texte* also denotes illustrations that are printed separately and then inserted into a book manuscript. The word thus refers to an element within a textual corpus that has an extra-textual status. By denying that there is any *hors-texte*, Derrida claims that no element within a text can be attributed status as extra-textual. Everything is equally textual. In the text there is no *hors-text*, no transcendental signified that binds the text to the "real world." The word "intertext" or even "implied context," i.e., a context that is embedded in a textual framework, would therefore be more accurate terms than "context" according to Derrida's line of thinking.

Derrida's no-outside-text-ontology is marginalized by those seeing the linguistic turn as an epistemological challenge. To claim that texts are not transparent is to admit that there is something outside that is more real and that it is the ultimate goal of interpretation to capture. To Derrida, there is only the text and that is more than enough. Texts are where history takes place. The linguistic turns represented by Darnton's ciritcs come in spite of individual differences all contradictory to Derrida's no-outside-text-ontology. By disputing the transparency of Darnton's source text, they all deny that the text is a proper mode of existence.

Derrida's Deconstructive Text Analysis

Derrida has been unwilling to describe deconstruction as a method because of the associations it gives regarding forcing a model on the text. We can nonetheless identify a reading strategy that often recurs in his analyses, yet is adapted to the distinctive character of the specific text. Using Derrida's reading of Descartes as a basis, his deconstructive text analysis can be described as a strategy in three stages:

– The first stage consists of identifying an utterance that provides access to the analysis—in this case the expression *sed forte*. Derrida frequently does not use a concept that is in the center of the argument as a starting point, but as peripheral concept that does not immediately capture the reader's attention. In the reading of Descartes, for example, this does not concern a philosophical expression that is specific to Descartes, but a small connecting word that is used in everyday language.

– The next stage consists of showing that there is a duality in the term that settles into the text's composition. In the reading of Descartes, focus is on the double meaning of *sed forte* as a "but" and a "but ... perhaps" that turns the counter argument into a hypothetical counter argument and the text into a discussion with an implied listener. The discourse therefore becomes not whole but dialogical. At this stage the difference between Derrida's reading strategy and that of Foucault becomes visible. Foucault treats the text as a complete system or *structure* of signs, while Derrida sees it as a signifying *process*.

– The third stage consists of showing how the text implies other texts or contexts in the form of genre, traditions, cultural codes and symbols. In the analysis of Descartes, on the one hand, the hyperbole and on the other the theosophical evidence provide such openings towards a larger text universe in terms of rhetorical genres, namely hyperbolic argumentation and scholastic writing tradition. However, the objective of this part of the analysis is not to identify these contexts but to show how they are played out and negotiated in a certain manner. The contexts that are brought in are premises rather than findings: they are the starting point rather than the final point of the analysis. In the analysis of Descartes, Derrida gives no detailed descriptions of the two writing traditions as phenomena outside the text as we could expect from a more traditional contextualization. He doesn't "leave" the text to study contexts but focuses on how they are implied and negotiated within the architecture of the text. It is how the contexts are handled in the text; the text's historical alchemy is Derrida's focus. This is where Derrida's approach takes a completely different turn from that of Foucault. Even if Foucault speaks about discourse and not prelinguistic realities, he treats this discourse as an *hors texte*. It is a transcendental signified, a macrostructure or a fixed point that the interpretation of Descartes text can lean on. For Foucault, the discourse is where interpretation stops and historiography reaches its final endpoint. For Derrida, it is rather where the play of signification sets off and historiography starts.

Drawing on Derrida's text-oriented methodology and ontology, in the last part of the article I will return to the Darnton debate. By confronting one of Darnton's readings with Derrida's deconstructive approach, I will try to answer the question I intimated in the introduction: What are the consequences for the analysis if the "little narrative" is not only considered the means but also as the goal of the study?

Darnton's Cats

Darnton's book bears the name of one of the six essays it contains on France under *l'ancien régime*. This title essay forms the basis for the further discussion of Darnton's understanding of text. In addition to being ascribed a special status through the choice of title, the essay can also be viewed as an exemplary expression of the anthropological perspective that Darnton describes in the introduction.

The narrative about the cats is set in a printing house in Paris in the first half of the eighteenth century. Darnton doesn't give much information about the text he is analyzing. However, we learn that it is drawn from the printer and former apprentice Nicolas Contat's memoirs, *Anecdotes typographiques*, written about twenty years after the events took place. In the printing house life as an apprentice was hard, Contat explains. There were two apprentice working there, Jérome (a fictionalized version of Contat) and Léveillé. The story tells how they, aided by the journeymen, took their revenge on the strict master family by torturing and killing their many cats, including the favourite cat of their mistress. They did it in a cunning manner: they clambered up on to the roof right over where the master and the mistress slept and made horrible catlike howls. They continued with this for several nights until the family began to worry that they were the victims of witchcraft and asked the men to get rid of the cats—except for the wife's favourite, *la grise*. The men used this as an excuse for initiating a ritual execution of all the cats—including *la grise*. This story was the object of great amusement at the time and became very popular. According to Darnton, to understand the narrative and its wide appeal it must be interpreted symbolically. At the beginning of the eighteenth century, the relationship between master and journeymen was characterized by a greater distance than previously. The journeymen were treated badly, while the master lived better. The masters also kept pets, particularly cats, which they treated better than the people who worked for them. By torturing the cats, and particularly the favourite of the master's wife, ordinary people were striking out at the family of the master on a symbolic level: the master's wife through insinuations of witchcraft and sexuality, and through their marriage also her husband. The narrative of the cat massacre can therefore be read as the journeymen's symbolic revolution against the master.

Darnton's essay falls into four major sections: First, he retells Contat's story as briefly resumed above. Second, he turns to the social political context and argues how different sources testify of increased distance between masters and journeymen in the first part of the eighteenth century. Large printing houses had eliminated most small shops. Statistics show, according to Darnton, that the number of masters declined while the number of journeymen remained stable which meant fewer printing houses with larger work forces. Darnton also claims that the journeymen were threatened from below by the so called *alloués*, which were unqualified printers that had not undergone the apprenticeship that allowed a journeyman to become master. They were therefore a symbol of a general tendency of labor becoming a commodity instead of a partnership, according to Darnton. In addition, sources also tell about changes in the masters' way of life characterized by laziness and luxury. All this motivates the journeymen's revolt against their master. But why cats?

The third part of Darnton's essay answers this question by turning to folklore and popular symbolism. Darnton points to how cat torture and cat killing formed part of carnival celebrations' reversal of social norms and of various religious ceremonies, both nationally and regionally (Darnton 1984, 83). The connection between cats and mysticism was also a well-known literary and artistic theme that had its roots as far back as ancient Egypt (Darnton 1984, 89). In addition, cats were associated with various forms of witchcraft, and both cats' body parts and cat excrement were key ingredients in popular medicine. The cat was also assigned a specific symbolic position in the household: it represented both a possible protector and a potential danger. Finally the cat was associated with sexuality and female fertility (Darnton 1984, 95). All this contributed in making cats into a powerful symbolic tool in the journeymen's revolution against their master. In the fourth and final part of his essay Darnton returns to the question of why the journeymen found the massacre so funny. They used the witch hunt as an excuse to murder the mistress' favorite cat and to insinuate that the mistress was herself a witch. In addition, they played on the connotations to sexuality in order to insult the wife for being adulterous and to mock the master as a cuckold. Not only did they hurt the master but they hurt him in a way that he did not fully understand because he was trapped within the symbolism without being conscious of it. He was therefore both made a cuckold and a fool.

Darnton's reading is interesting in a deconstructive perspective since it is based on an apparently simple and unambigious sign, namely "the cat." It also shows how this sign is the carrier of an intricate symbolism. Complex cultural contradictions are reflected in the relations to cats. Viewed in this way, Darnton's reading corresponds well with the first stage of Derrida's reading strategy where what seem to be peripheral or unproblematic text elements are made into the focus of the analysis. In a sense, "the cat" also functions as an opening towards a larger text universe that Derrida finds in Descartes's hyperbolic *sed forte*. In keeping with what I have described as the third stage of Derrida's reading strategy, Darnton views the narrative about the cat massacre not only against the backdrop of social structures but analyses how traditions and cultural symbolism are reiterated in the narrative. When Darnton focuses on these traditions, however, it is not as rhetorical devices within the text. The contexts are *hors-textes* to Darnton. In order to study them he leaves the textual framework. He is not concerned with what happens in the text but with what the text says about what is happening outside. More specifically he draws on the various contexts to confirm an interpretation that has already been made. The tradition material is used to substantiate the conflicts between master and journeyman. Is it thus possible to reopen Darnton's closed hermeneutical circle and read the tradition material on cats into the narrative in another way? Are there historical negotiations taking place in the narrative about the cats that Darnton with his outside-text-contextualization does not notice?

As Darnton sees it, the narrative's symbolism is based on a contrast in the attitude to cats between the master and the journeymen: while for the master's family the cat is a human-like creature, for the journeymen it is only an animal. "Keeping pets was as alien to the workers as torturing animals was to the bourgeois," he writes (Darnton 1984, 100). However, Darnton's analysis does not provide clear evidence for such a difference in attitude. On one hand, the master's reaction when he sees the slaughtered cats bears witness to the fact that he is far from viewing them as people or is shaken about the way they have been treated: he accuses the men of spending their time killing cats instead of working. On the other hand, the apprentices themselves in a way treat the cats as human beings through the solemn ritual heresy trials they put them through. Moreover, Darnton's own presentation of the tradition material demonstrates that torturing cats and anthropomorphizing them are actually connected. The indefinable *je ne sais quoi* of the cat, the mystical "something" that has resulted in thoughts of sorcery, witchcraft and devilry, stems precisely from the cat's quasi-human characteristics and from the idea of a mystical relationship between the cat and human beings: "One can mistake a cat's howl at night for a human scream, torn from some deep, visceral part of man's animal nature" (Darnton 1984, 89). The connection between the two attitudes is also expressed in the narrative: the master's family treats their cats as people while *at the same time* associating them with witchcraft and sorcery. Thoughts of witchcraft are what come to their minds when they hear the false cat howls at night, and that is why they allow the cats to be killed.

Darnton's interpretation is also based on another assumption: the apprentices themselves do not believe in the cat symbolism but use it as a deliberate tool in a kind of social struggle against the master's family. He claims that they control their cultural grammar with the same ease as the poet controls language. In contrast, the master's family are superstitious and therefore let themselves be frightened by the cat howls, but the master does not have sufficient distance from the tradition material to enable him to *see* the symbolic game that is being played against him. Viewed in this manner, it is in fact the bourgeoisie who represent popular culture. However, this assumption is not clear either, and can be said to deconstruct itself: if the advanced symbolism Darnton shows by his analysis is to have an effect, i.e., to make the master feel concerned, he must be able to *understand* the insinuations—that his wife is associated with a cat, with a witch and with sexuality. He must thus have a certain distance to the symbolism. On their part the apprentices cannot be said to stand completely *outside* the symbol tradition: the narrative opens with the apprentices being prevented from sleeping because some cats "were celebrating the witches' Sabbath" all night. The expression bears witness to an insider attitude to the symbolism.

For Darnton the narrative's popularity and general appeal provides evidence to interpret it as a conscious symbolic rebellion. The audience delights in the narrative because it conveys a hidden ideological message from the apprentices who take part in the plot to recipients of the same standing. However, the social symbolism is not necessarily a prerequisite for the entertainment value of the narrative. When the narrative made people laugh, it could well be because the men made the master's actions turn against him: he himself contributed to legitimizing the cat massacre. This can be interpreted as a form of dramatic irony that was a well-known technique in classic dramas (Attardo 2000), and that can therefore not simply be seen as an expression of a time-specific social project. Moreover, it is important to distinguish between the anecdote's *narrator* and the *actors* who take part in the plot. Even though the narrator presents the events as if they were governed by an inner logic— from the first imitated cat howl to the massacre—these events need not have been intentional on the part of the actors. The problem with Darnton's analysis is that he draws conclusions about the story (the events the narrative refers to) based on the narrative (the linguistic presentation) (Genette 1988).

Chartier (1985) puts forward a similar objection to Darnton: he claims that Darnton draws conclusions from text to incidents before he has considered the text's specific function and distinctive character. Darnton draws hasty conclusions about the reality behind the text, Chartier claims. My objection is both more serious and less serious than Chartier's: in my opinion the problem with Darnton's analysis is not that he draws too hasty conclusions about reality, but that he does not include the text in his understanding of reality. Only the story is real for Darnton, not the narrative. The narrative has no ontological status; it is the story that is the object of the study. He therefore does not devote any separate attention to the play of signification in the text.

The Cat Symbolism and the Text's Production of Meaning

It is at this point—the second stage of Derrida's reading strategy—that Darnton's analysis particularly deviates from a deconstructive text analysis. From a deconstructive perspective the cat in the narrative cannot be interpreted as a weapon in a socio-political conflict that one party sees and uses and that the other party is a blind victim of. An interpretation of this kind reduces the complexity of the cat symbolism in the text's production of meaning. For Darnton the central concept of the analysis—the cat—stands as a clear and unproblematic element in the cultural grammar that the narrative reflects. The cultural grammar outside the text is used to clarify the interpretation of the signifying process within the text—just as Foucault "clarifies" Descartes's section on madness through reference to the prevailing social discourse.

However, as with Descartes's *sed forte*, it can be claimed that the cat plays an ambiguous role in the narrative Darnton analyzes. The cat is part of the social struggle that the text conveys. The journeymen take their revenge on the master by killing his cats. At the same time the cat does not function as a fixed sign in the text but as an opening towards a complex and opaque intertextual universe. This universe cannot be reduced to a social tool in the hands of one of the protagonists in the narrative. Both the social positions in the narrative—in spite of their conflicting interests—are based on the fact that they partly identify themselves with and partly distance themselves from the cat symbolism. The dynamics of the narrative rest on the fact that the master and the journeymen regard cats as both human-like creatures and *only* as cats, and that they believe in the connection between cats and witchcraft at the same time as they do *not* believe in it. As they are portrayed in the narrative, both master *and* journeymen stand outside and inside the symbolism. Otherwise the narrative would collapse. The contrast between master and journeymen is dependent on a unified view of the cat's symbolic importance.

It is equally important that it is not the individuals behind the narrative that are governed by this symbolism. It is only the narrative we have access to. We cannot know which cultural grammar may have controlled the events that are referred to and whether these events have occurred in exactly this way. The object of both Darnton's analysis and my own Derrida-inspired critique is relational textual positions rather than persons. Darnton (1984, 78) himself is also quick to admit that the text cannot be read as a mirror of real events: "...it cannot be regarded as a mirror-image of what actually happened." However, this conclusion does not appear to have consequences for his reading. Viewed from Derrida's theoretical standpoint, where there is no outside-text, the implication will be that both the master and the journeymen must be regarded as "actants" acting on the basis of their place in the text and not intentional actors (Greimas 1983). It is the place that "master" and "journeyman" are assigned in the eighteenth-century text that we must analyze, not their general role in French social life in that century.

However, this does imply that the text cannot provide access to cultural processes that are larger than the individual text. But instead of reading from the text and outwards to a social macrostructure (Darnton) or discourse (Foucault), we must focus on the cultural negotiations that are taking place at the textual level. The concrete text is a place where cultural categories are negotiated in a dialogue with diverse symbolic and intertextual input. It is a part of a continuously active intertextual weave. So how does this intertextual weave work in the narrative Darnton analyzes?

As Darnton (1984, 78–79) points out, the narrative creates on the one hand a clear contrast between master and workers: "Contat [the narrator] set the event in the context of remarks about the disparity between the lot of workers and the bourgois—a matter of the basic elements in life: work, food and sleep." The relationship to cats is part of this disparity since the master's family treats the cats better than the journeymen. On the other hand, the symbolism the cats are associated with is a language that unites the two actants and that governs how they act towards each other. It is a joint intertextual reference that makes the text's two social positions possible. The picture the narrative creates of master and journeymen as antagonistic positions rests on an assumption that they have a common set of intertextual references consisting of carnival rituals, religious celebrations etc. where the connection between cats and magic plays a role. The social struggle the text stages takes place on the premise of a cultural symbolism that they have in common. The two positions could not be played out so sharply vis-à-vis each other in the text if they did not share a common cultural capital.

The text's historical significance stems from the fact that it constitutes two positions—master and journeyman—that cannot solely be understood as rank or class positions that are opposed to each other but also as *intertextual positions* that are almost identical. Cats are part of both what splits them socially and what binds them together intertextually. What is interesting is that the intertextual positions in a way deconstruct the social positions that are set against each other in the text. Master and journeymen are not as different as one first thought.

Thus the text that Darnton analyzes gives no grounds for viewing the cat exclusively as a symbol of a greater distance between master and journeyman in eighteenth-century France, or as a weapon in a social struggle between them. Contrary to Darnton's purpose, the reference to the tradition material does not help to emphasize the distance between the two actors. In fact the opposite is the case: the narrative bears witness to the fact that the cat symbolism is something that both parties are part of and that unites them at the deepest level. The parties stand closer to each other in attitude than Darnton's analysis testifies to.

The fact that both parties are concerned about the tradition material contributes to deconstructing a dichotomist notion of two separate cultures where the ordinary people stand on one side and the elite on the other, each with their own set of cultural references. If one dares to open the narrative of the cat massacre to competition from the traditions that Darnton himself describes, this creates problems for Darnton's cultural grammar. The cat symbolism does not confirm the relationship between the microstructure and the macrostructure—it distorts it. The text is the stage for complex intertextual references where master and journeyman are played out against each other and are united through their relationship to cats.

The Text and Reality

In a way, Darnton represents a linguistic turn by being more concerned with stories and symbols than with ideas or events. He also emphasizes that the text does not offer us direct access to historical elements, but that we are at the mercy of the narrator's language and interpretations. But even so, Darnton keeps language and text outside the study's object: the reality that he tries to capture lies behind the text, not in the narrative that is analyzed. The result is that he is subject to the same criticism that Derrida directs at Foucault—he does not see what happens in the text. The historical negotiations that take place within the text's own universe, where the cats play a significant though ambiguous role, hence fall outside the focus of the analysis. His interpretation therefore points to a clearer distance in the relationship between master and journeymen than what is actually conveyed through the narrative.

I thus agree with Chartier, LaCapra and Mah that Darnton does not pay enough attention to texts but I disagree on the nature of the problem. Even if their linguistic turn is more radical than that of Darnton, it remains epistemological. All three claim that Darnton reads too much history into his source text. The problem is, according to the three critics that Darnton doesn't take into account that the text he is analyzing is not a transparent expression of real events but a linguistic interpretation. Seen this way, one way of solving this problem would be to admit that every historical account is polluted by language and that no interpretation is more accurate than the other. Another solution would be to propose a reading that by being more sensitive to the text is meant to capture the reality behind more accurately. The first solution is relativist, the second essentialist (no less than Darnton's own interpretation). I am not comfortable with either of these solutions. The essentialist approach undermines, on the one hand, that history takes place within the text. History is not outside or transcendent to the textual structure but part of the textual architecture. The historical alchemy of a specific text is thus not only the route to historical analysis but its final end.

On the other hand, the relativist approach underestimates the fact that texts are real. They are positively given. Texts are not reflections of historical reality but they are historical reality. They are scenes of specific cultural encounters and negotiations that can be observed and studied.

Rather than Darnton's historical ethnography, I propose a historiography of texts. Contrary to the approach of Darnton and his critics, a historiography of texts would not promote attentiveness to texts in order to capture "reality" more adequately. Attentiveness to text is motivation in itself. This is ultimately because texts should be considered as scenes and not as sources of history.

References

Ankersmit, F., and H. Kellner. 1995. *A New Philosophy of History*. Chicago: University of Chicago Press.

Attardo, S. 2000. "Irony as Relevant Inappropriateness." *Journal of Pragmatics* 32, no. 6: 793–826.

Berkhofer, R. F. 1995. *Beyond the Great Story: History as Text and Discourse*. Cambridge, MA: Harvard University Press.

Chartier, R. 1985. "Text, Symbols, and Frenchness." *Journal of Modern History* 57, no. 9: 682–95.

Darnton, R. 1984. *The Great Cat Massacre and Other Episodes in French Cultural History*. New York: Basic Books.

Derrida, J. 1967. *L'écriture et la différence*. Paris: Seuil.

———. 1969. *De la grammatologie*. Paris: Minuit.

Descartes, R. 2008. *Discourse on the Method and the Meditations*. New York: Cosimo Classics.

Fernandez, J. 1988. "Historians Tell Tales: Of Cartesian Cats and Gallic Cock-fights." *Journal of Modern History* 60, no. 1: 113–27.

Foucault, M. 1972. *Histoire de la folie à l'âge classique* [second edition with preface and appendix 'La folie, l'absence d'œuvre' and 'Mon corps, ce papier, ce feu']. Paris: Gallimard.

Genette, G. 1988. *Narrative Discourse Revisited*. New York: Cornell University Press.

Greimas, AJ. 1983. *Structural Semantics: An Attempt at a Method*. Nebraska: University of Nebraska Press.

Jenkins, K. 1991. *Re-thinking History*. London: Routledge.

———. 1997. *The Postmodern History Reader*. New York: Routledge.

———. 1999. *Why History: Ethics and Postmodernity*. London: Routledge.

Kirby, A. 2006. "The Death of Postmodernism and Beyond." *Philosophy Now* 58.

LaCapra, D. 1988. "Chartier, Darnton, and the Great Symbol Massacre." *Journal of Modern History* 60, no. 1: 95–112.

Mah, H. 1999. "Suppressing the Text: The Metaphysics of Ethnographic History in Darnton's Great Cat Massacre." *History Workshop Journal* 31, no. 1: 1–26.

Mortimer, I. 2008. "'What Isn't History?' The Nature and Enjoyment of History in the Twenty-First century." *History* 93, no. 312: 454–74.

Munslow, A. 1997. *Deconstructing History*. London: Routledge.

Schaanning, E. 1997. *Vitenskap som skapt viten*. Oslo: Spartacus.

White, H. 1973. *Metahistory: The Historical Imagination in Nineteeth-Century Europe.* Baltimore: Johns Hopkins University Press.

Zagorin P. 1999. "History, the Referent, and Narrative: Reflections on Postmodernism Now." *History and Theory* 1: 1–24.

www.ingramcontent.com/pod-product-compliance
Lightning Source LLC
Chambersburg PA
CBHW021002150626
46549CB00012BA/943